Success in Regional and Multi Unit Management

PRELUDE

Since writing my first book Success in Auto Body and Collision Shop management much has changed in my career and in the industry itself. In this my second book I look at things more from the perspective of a regional or district manager or above who is engaged in multi-unit management. Starting off with belief and vision and then spending many pages on leadership. The older I get, the more I am convinced that success for yourself and for your team comes down to leadership. It comes down to you. Unfortunately, that is exactly what we are lacking in much of our world today. It is my hope that this book and my experiences will help you as they have me. I have grown as a leader sometimes the hard way through challenges and failures, but I am nothing but thankful for them as they have helped shape me for the leader I am today.

The thoughts that I share with you in this book are mine alone and not the thoughts of any company that I have worked for past or present. Also, I have done my best to accurately remember the situations talked about in this book. If I made a mistake, it was simply due to the passage of time and not on purpose. No book is ever complete, and I am sure that I will notice, and you may too that I may not have included things that I should have included or put things in that I should have left out. I have been working on this book for several years and feel it is ready to be shared.

I am humbled that you decided to buy this book and spend some time with me as I share my journey with you.

DEDICATION

This book is dedicated to the many talented people that I have had the joy to work with in the many years in the collision repair industry.

THE IMPORTANCE OF BELIEF AND VISION

Suppose you wish to be successful in any undertaking, whether it be business or in your personal life. In that case, you must begin by believing that your undertaking is possible, and that success will be yours. Your intentions and work ethic, of course, are essential and are necessary. However, if you do not genuinely believe with all your heart that your undertaking will succeed, you will fail or fall short no matter how hard you try.

Several times, I have been put in charge of leading a failing or underperforming department or business and turning it around to success. I have often wondered how or why the former management did not make the changes I made to turn the operation in the right direction, as the answers seemed obvious, and the changes were easy to make.

With hindsight, I have found that they could have turned things around with simple changes and a short amount of time for the desired effect. I did not overhaul the entire operation or find some complex answer that no one else could have figured out. I just stepped in, observed, and made the necessary decisions and changes that needed to be made. To me, they seemed obvious. But I know that I was totally and utterly committed to the success of my enterprise, and I would not consider failure as an option, not for one minute.

I also believe in myself and what effect I have on the situation without being egotistical about it. I think this is where you must start to be successful in authoring this book with multi-unit managers in mind. No matter how good your plan may be, it will not be successful without a sharp vision and a genuine belief in it.

Know that you will succeed

The main difference between the approach that I used, and the one former management used was that I knew that I would succeed and that nothing would stop me from obtaining the goal that I had set. In my mind, the slate was clean, and nothing was off the table regarding solutions and possibilities. I could see where I wanted the operation to go; I visualized the outcome before I started. I could see the result I was looking for as if it were present at that very moment.

Once you can see what you are trying to accomplish, it is just a matter of connecting the dots from where you are to where you are trying to go. If you were planning a trip with your family, you would know your destination before you pack up the car and start driving, wouldn't you? Over and over, I have been shown that the first step to success is believing it is possible. Not only believing but also seeing a clear picture of what it looks like. How can you do this? It is simpler than you think. It just takes the proper perspective.

First, it is essential to ensure you are stepping back and can see the forest from the trees. The closer you are to the situation, the less clear the picture will be for you and the more emotional your reaction might be.

Detach Yourself And Step Back

The closer you are to the front lines of an operation, the more likely you will not see the overall picture and the possibilities available to you, hence your ability to change things. Unfortunately, at times, the front line becomes your reality, and you may not be able to see a different avenue to take. You may become a reactor to situations instead of an actor steering the ship to its destination.

Therefore, someone in your department or organization must be far enough away from the day-to-day operations and struggle to see the large-scale picture clearly and from a strategic and unemotional point of view. This is a crucial point to being a multi-unit manager or above. Please do not allow yourself to be swayed by everyday problems, as they may sway your judgment. If you are the only option and cannot turn over the day-to-day operations to someone else, you can still be the "thinker" too.

However, you will have to find time to go to a quiet place without disturbance to think of how to improve your daily operations. This action pays dividends and is essential to your long-term success. It does not matter how you do it; it is just that you do it. Whether taking time away to find a place of solitude to think about or just locking yourself in a room without distraction. The important part is to detach yourself and look at things from an unbiased perspective. Just you, your mind, and the ability to write things down really helps me.

Realizing the critical factor of staying detached directly from the front lines is essential. You may sometimes need to go in yourself to cover a position or help one of the businesses you oversee. However, I caution you to be careful and get back in your position as soon as possible so you can see the entire strategic picture. While working on the front lines, you may become emotionally compromised by a person or a situation.

An example of this could be my wife and kids working for the same company I work for. They do not directly report to me, and for good reason. No matter how hard I try, I am emotionally compromised when it comes to them, and my love for them will not allow me to be impartial. Comparably, if you work on the front lines, you see and relate to the everyday challenges too closely. You may start to make excuses for mediocre performance that are just crutches and excuses. An example might be, "Well, you just don't understand the customers and how unreasonable they are here in Anytown USA; they just can't be satisfied." As a successful leader, accepting statements like that does nothing but harm to everyone. It allows the team to use that crutch and excuse instead of drilling down to what can be accomplished. If you are too close to the action, you may buy excuses like that. You must take the time to isolate and detach yourself and think and plan in an environment free of distraction.

Map out your business and its operations from both the

customer's and business perspectives, and take it step by step, carefully noting how it should flow. Be sure to note differences in your mind regarding how it flows now compared to how it should flow. Now, think of ideas and changes you can institute to bring the current state closer to how things should be on paper. You may need to make process, personnel, and facility changes. Depending on the current state you are working in, it will usually depend on how far away you are from where you want to be. Suppose you are tasked with fixing a severely broken operation. In that case, you may want to start with just one or two significant changes you can make today that will immediately and positively impact the business. Then, once those changes are made and the business pivots in the right direction, you can reassess and produce the following one or two things. The basics would be a good place if you are unsure where to start.

The Danger Of Being Too Close

My dad told me something when I was younger that I didn't understand in the beginning. "You can't be friends with your employees, but you can be a friendly boss." The hard part is that you spend most of your time with the people at work, and it's easy to form bonds of friendship that extend out of work. I've learned the hard way that it is better to keep your friends as your friends and your coworkers as coworkers.

The reason is that there are times when people only want to be your friend outside of work for their gain. Unfortunately, I've seen people who grew from coworkers to friends disappear when the relationship didn't benefit them anymore by being my friend. The hard part for me is that I am not built that way, and If I consider you a friend, it's not to gain something from you, and I just don't shut off our friendship because I feel like it. So, it's sad that some people only want to be your friend while there is something there for them to gain. Another pitfall is that people think the rules don't apply to them because they are your friends.

It's tough for some to believe they must hold to the same standards as everyone else because they feel your friendship gives them special privileges. It's a shame because, if anything, I expect more from my friends, and I hold them to an even higher standard than everyone else. I'm the reverse of some; kissing up to me has no effect. Again, you must exceed expectations and be more effective and successful than the rest to impress me. An example of how this can hurt a leader is one I will share with you next.

A general manager was running one of my smaller locations. He was thoughtful and knew what it takes to run a successful collision repair shop. He had all the knowledge and training that was necessary. However, he didn't always apply it. There were times when he showed flashes of success, and I was encouraged. Then, he would follow it up by showing stretches where he would allow failure on the most essential things. I began to hear rumblings he was getting too close to the other employees in the shop. This included socializing with them regularly and going to long lunches during the day with them. I warned him and even shared my dad's quote, precisely what he should avoid. Things continued a negative trajectory, and other employees started to complain and even accuse him of engaging in activities he should not have been during the workday.

Remember, this manager had the talent and the skills. However, even though he was warned, his performance continued to slide. How can you hold your team accountable if you go out and party with them? Well, you can't, and that was part of the problem. No one was accountable for anything, and it became a chaotic situation. I even scheduled a call with him and his office team to level-set everyone and get everyone on the right page. I also saw this as an opportunity to help the manager get things back under control as I opened the door for him to walk through. Well, guess how that worked out? Not too well, as only two members of his office staff showed up to the call. Guess where the other three members, including himself, were? They were out for a long lunch and weren't even at the shop, so he forgot about the call. So, the very thing that was the problem and the reason that I was having the call in the first place was what he was doing. Unfortunately, after this blatant disregard of policy, I was forced to remove him as the manager. We still talk to him to this day, and he has moved on to another organization where he seems successful. Maybe he needed this situation as a wake-up call, and hopefully, he learned something from it. When you sign up to be a leader, you can't just be one of the boys or girls anymore. It would be best if you held yourself to a higher standard. You sign up for this when you agree to become a leader.

The Answer May Be More Straightforward Than You Think

It may be overstated, but how often have you heard the term "we need to get back to the basics." I am sure you have heard the saying several times, too. It almost seems like a pre-canned answer without substance. However, I have found that while it may sound too simple to be accurate, most of the time, there is value to it. Here is one advantage to getting back to basics. If you are faced with an operation that needs improvement, an excellent place to start is with the fundamental tasks that your business performs. Instead of having to fix twelve different things, by getting the basic core tasks you perform, and if done right, you may fix several things by focusing on a handful of things done right. Regarding body shop terms, start with complete disassembly and accurate estimates first. This would fix so many problems down the line that it would have taken you longer and consumed more effort if you had done it by attacking everything at once.

It may even be more straightforward than that. You may need to start with cleaning up and organizing your shop. One of my shops struggled about a year ago, and many things needed attention. I grabbed a broom and started sweeping the floor and cleaning up. Why? Because it needed to be done, and I am not above it, that is where I started. It helped the business's overall appearance and set the tone that I was there to help and be a part of the solution. Soon, others joined me without asking, and we were off in a positive direction. Before that moment, there was finger-pointing and fighting among the team. After that moment, people were helping clean up and carry out the trash. Sometimes, the beginning of the answer starts simply like that.

If Your Vision Is Pessimistic, So Will Your Results

Also, be mindful of not allowing your mind to be influenced by unproven preconceived notions or by having small goals. Preconceived notions can have a debilitating effect on any operation or leader. As the leader, you cannot fall into these self-defeating traps. A few years ago, I was tasked with working with and trying to help a struggling manager. When I first met him, I was struck immediately by his outward negativity. Everywhere he looked, and every sentence out of his mouth was negative. He pointed the finger everywhere: the facility, area, staff, equipment, and former managers. He pointed the finger in every direction except where it truly belonged to him.

Even though I was there to help him, he was reluctant and did not want me around. In the end, unbeknownst to him, he was the real issue. He was the real reason the shop was in trouble because of his negativity, finger-pointing, and lack of leadership and ownership.

The words that came out of his mouth became his truth and his worldview, and hence his reality and the reality of everyone else. I took command of his shop and wiped the slate clean. Everything and everyone got a fresh start with me, and I told everyone so. They all knew where the actual issue was and were happy to go in a new direction.

In a matter of days, and with the same people, equipment, and everything else, this shop turned around and performed much improved. There was nothing wrong with any of the things that the former manager pointed his finger at. By his highly negative nature and speech, he spoke and manifested failure into existence because that is what he believed. His view and words took something that nothing was wrong with and made it bad, just like he said.

On the contrary, my positive view and outlook generated a feeling of success and possibility. Even in multi-unit management, spotting a "leader" who behaves this way is easy. I put a leader in quotes because the only place they will lead their team is a failure. These are the managers who, when on calls or in meetings, are constantly firing off complaints and reasons why something cannot be done. Why? What is to be gained by acting that way? Instead of complaining, why not figure out ways to overcome the obstacles and lead your team to success? Sometimes, I wonder if they are paying attention and hearing themselves and the negativity and self-defeating talk coming out of their mouths. Not only does it stop them from accomplishing anything. But it also prevents their team from accomplishing anything. It also takes time away from those who want to move forward and achieve the mission. So do not complain; be a leader and a difference-maker. I have repeatedly said this in my career: the leader makes all the difference.

This is where being careful of preconceived notions comes in.

What if I, as the Regional Manager, had taken this General Manager's feedback as gospel and believed everything he had to say? If I had, I would have read the situation completely wrong and may have acted in the wrong way and against the wrong people. Had I done so, I would have eliminated the good people who were working hard instead of the individual who was creating the problems. An old proverb states, "One look is worth a thousand reports." In layperson's terms, it is better to go and look at the situation with your own eyes and ears than to rely on someone else's reports. This rings true in multi-unit management as well.

Everyone has their perspective, which drives their view on things whether they realize it or not. Their report might be correct. Then again, it might not be. The only way for you to know is for you to investigate the situation yourself before you decide. If you only hear one side of the story, you will likely follow that preconceived notion and choose based on insufficient data. If you are not careful, you will add to the problem, and people will lose faith in your leadership. The more critical the decision, the more important it is to investigate it more thoroughly and possibly from different angles.

Have An Open Mind

Your words and your beliefs are potent tools. Use them wisely; you can help quickly turn a challenging situation into a good one with minimal effort. The most crucial factor here that will lead to success is for you, as the creator of this plan, to have an open mind and believe that success will be attained. This belief must be honest, and it must be unshakable. Without it, you are destined to fail, and there will be no chance of success. As soon as you allow doubt to creep into your mind, it is like a crack in a foundation wall, and in time, it will get worse and cause the entire building to fail.

First, have an unshakable faith in your success, then plan what needs to be done, execute your plan, and finally, always be fluid and ready to make improvements and changes as the situation dictates. Your plan must be a starting point and open to change as the situation changes. Do not waiver or be stuck if your initial changes do not get you exactly where you need to go. In that case, take another look at where you are and produce a new plan with changes.

There is a term called having a plan with branches. Imagine a tree with all its branches; your strategy should look like a tree with all its branches spreading out with different possibilities and actions. As your plan develops, it also spreads out with different viable solutions and changes, like the branches of a tree would. Your plan and vision should not be a straight line; they should include all the different branches, avenues, and possibilities that could happen as you make changes in your operation. I am sure you have heard the saying play chess, not checkers. It is the same idea: plan with preparation in mind what could happen with each of your moves, the possibilities that could follow, and your countermoves.

You may have also heard about "if, then." If this happens, I will do this, or if that happens, my move will be this. Unfortunately, many people do not have a plan, let alone one with different possibilities. Without a plan, you may be tempted to react with emotion. Reacting with emotion is never good when you are a manager and a leader. Without a plan, you may decide that it was a mistake when looked at afterward. With a plan in place, you will be less inclined to react emotionally because it does not follow along with the plan. If you have a plan with branches, you would have already planned out the different possibilities and outcomes that could come with each move you make and be prepared for it.

However, you can still be thrown a curveball even with a solid plan with different outcomes.

It Is Ok To Pivot

In life, nothing is guaranteed, and nothing is for sure. So, even with the best and most well-thought-out plan, you cannot be ready for everything. Sometimes, unexpected and unplanned stuff happens. Remember, your plan is your starting point, and planning effectively is time well spent. But there are times when the best-laid plans cannot be ready for a possibility you were not planning.

Here is an example: You have a seasoned employee you are counting on to be a part of your operation for the long term. Hence, you had no plan in place as you thought they were not someone you had to plan to leave. Then, unexpectedly, they tell you that their spouse accepted a job in another part of the country, and they are moving in two weeks. An event like this was not planned for and may throw many of your other plans into disarray. Well, you can do nothing other than scrap the former plans and produce a new one. As information changes, your plans will have to change as well. The exercise and thought process of creating a plan is often needed. You may not refer to the plan, but the time you spend thinking about it is good exercise and may be all you need. The more you think about things, the quicker you will be able to react, and the faster ideas will come to your mind.

Vision

A Google search says that the definition of vision is the ability to think about or plan the future with imagination or wisdom. Both in your life and in your business, it is of the utmost importance that you have a vision. Just like you do not get into a car before knowing your destination, you cannot be effective in life or business without having a vision.

A vision is your destination and the target of where you are trying to go. Without a vision or, in this example, a destination, you would be just moving, but it could be just in circles. There's movement, so it looks like something is happening, but you are not getting closer to your destination because you do not know where that destination is. To be truly effective, you must have a vision and a destination for where you are trying to get to. Not only that but the more significant your vision is, the bigger you can create your reality.

A simple example is the mighty and powerful elephant held in place by a small stake in the ground. If only the elephant had the vision to pull the stake out of the ground, he could do it quickly. However, the elephant's vision is small, and he does not even try. Yes, that is an oversimplified example, but the same idea holds for us as humans in our business and personal lives. There are two different problems that I most often see: a lack of vision and a small vision. As stated above, some people have no vision or destination in mind. Rise daily and go through the motions with no destination in mind.

Each of us has a basis for our vision, usually built upon our experiences and history. There is a tendency for us as humans to see things only through the lens of what we have experienced and what we have seen to be true. An easy example of this is if you have always worked in small businesses and have only ever seen a store deliver $200,000.00 in sales maximum in a month, which is all you have ever seen. There would be a tendency for you to have that number as a ceiling of possibilities because you have never seen more than that done before.

As I have been managing businesses for almost thirty years, I have seen hundreds of different companies my career has taken me past. I have also seen and been a part of working with some of the most aggressive and successful businesses in the Philadelphia area. Hence, when I view a shop, I look at it against some of the most profitable shops in the industry. Someone who has not seen the success and the shops I have may look at the shop and not even think what I have in my head is possible. That is my advantage; I come in ready to make the shop as big or better than some shops I have seen in my career. Had I only worked in one shop my entire life, that would be all I would know and most likely be unable to imagine more than what I had seen and experienced with my own two eyes.

Vision is a continuous process. As time moves on and situations change, so can your vision. A good exercise is to find a quiet place and take a moment to review your goals, what you want your goals to be, and what you want your vision to be for your businesses. Why? Because of what your goals formerly were, you may have accomplished them and need to readjust and shoot higher. In the same way, you may have set the bar too high, and the team is losing faith that they can accomplish it. Take the time to review your vision and regularly update it. You are looked upon to set and believe in the vision as a leader. You should believe in it more than anyone else and be unshakable with your faith. Your team will see if you are not one hundred percent bought in. Your faith in your vision might be the thing that gets it through to the finish line.

Lastly, but most importantly, you need to believe in yourself. As I think about it, I can honestly say that I have seen many good and capable people who had all the tools they needed to succeed, except for one thing: they did not believe in themselves. When this happens and people do not believe in themselves, they freeze in place. Once this happens, they sit in place, waiting for someone to come and save them. Like the elephant, they can easily take the required actions to get moving, but they do not. People would be unstoppable if they just took simple action and believed in themselves. To me, this is a heartbreaking thing to witness.

Being detached and seeing everything happening gives me the perspective of the possibilities as a leader. The sad thing is that they had all the tools at their disposal; they did not believe enough in themselves to complete it. It did not come automatically to me, but I believe in myself to an exceedingly high degree. How high? What would I do if I were on an airplane in an emergency and they wanted to see who could land the plane? I would look around, and if no one jumped up and said they were a pilot, I would raise my hand and get in the pilot's seat. What is the difference between me and a commercial pilot? The commercial pilot has the training and the tools. If I had the tools and the training, I could pilot a commercial jet, too.

So, no matter what you are doing or engaging in, to work toward believing in yourself, you need to put the work in. How much time do you devote to your craft? Do you hold yourself to the highest standards? Are you taking time to learn and grow to be the best "whatever your position is" you can be? If so, congratulations because no one is coming to save you; it is up to you. If you are not taking the time, why aren't you? For what are you waiting? Life is not a sit-down dinner; it is a buffet, and you need to get out of your seat and get it; if you act, if you put the work in, your faith in yourself will increase. It is that easy; what are you waiting for?

The second most important question asked in most panel interviews that I have sat on is, "What are you doing for your personal development?" Unfortunately, I have often seen a look of fear come across the face of the candidate at this point. Usually, they struggle and say, " Well, I haven't had time for personal development. At that point, someone who may have been winning the interview is put back on their heels and in a defensive position. Here is the thing: we all have the same amount of time, and no one gets more than the twenty-four hours allotted. It is what you do with them that counts.

I recently finished a meeting with my regional managers and asked what they were currently doing for personal development. One responded aggressively that he did not have time and was defensive when I said he should make the time. He reacted angrily, saying I do not have time to read books. I shared some easy and actual examples of what I was doing for my personal development. First, I love to read and use any chance I can, even if it is just ten minutes to read a book. But that is not enough, so I also buy audiobooks on Audible and use what could be useless time in the car to listen to a book, sometimes with the authors themselves speaking. So, instead of listening to something useless like sports radio, I turned that into valuable learning time by listening to audiobooks. I then shared with him that most mornings, as I eat breakfast or drink coffee, I have my laptop open to a podcast or a learning class. There are several choices available from LinkedIn Learning, Coursera, or others that I can use to take more useless time and turn into helpful time. After sharing this with him, I believe I struck a nerve, and he saw that there were other possibilities, and I hope you do, too.

Before you start making changes or doing things, you need to know where you are trying to go. If you start before you know where you are going, you just might go in circles and waste time or get burned out or frustrated. Before you start think and plan first. Consider the what ifs and the possibilities so that when you hit a roadblock or a challenge, you already have a contingency plan for that. Like Mike Tyson said everyone has a plan until they get punched in the mouth. Well, you should have had a plan for that and considered that contingency if you were facing off against

Iron Mike.

The Extra Mile

1. You must not just believe but know that you will succeed.
2. If you are too close, detach to see a more comprehensive view.
3. The answer or the first thing you should do may be more straightforward than you think.
4. You can't simultaneously have a pessimistic vision and a positive result.
5. Have an open mind.
6. Like Ross said, "pivot." (Friends reference)

DESIRE AND DISCIPLINE

I was recently watching a short YouTube video on Michael Jordan. In the era when I was growing up, there was no greater basketball player than Michael. However, his raw skills did not impress me the most, even though he certainly had a great deal of that. It was his desire and his discipline that impressed me most. The reason I am interested in Michael was not his God-given talent; it was the fact he drove himself hard even when he could have taken the effortless way out. His desire to make practices as hard as actual games is legendary and the discipline he demanded of himself and his teammates each day has been well documented. There are many examples of talented people who did not have the desire or the discipline. An easy example of that is Allen Iverson, who gave the famous speech about "practice." How much more could Allen Iverson have accomplished if he coupled his talent with desire and discipline? More importantly, how much more can you accomplish with them?

Roadblocks

I will start this by asking you a question that I often ask my team members. What are you waiting for? Followed by who or what is stopping you from attaining your goals? I have followed a simple recipe for many years, and it has proven correct repeatedly. When I start collaborating with a new team or business, I always ask the same question. What roadblocks are stopping you from success? Whatever they are, let me know, and I will manage them for you. Is it a piece of equipment? Let me know, and I will take care of it. Is there a problem with the facility that you have been unable to get fixed? Bring it to me, and I will see it through. Then, I will stand true to my word and do whatever it takes to manage those items.

Then I will come back and say, now that I have taken care of such and such, what else is holding you back? Invariably, they will produce another item that is smaller than the first. So, I repeat the process; I will make sure that I do whatever it takes to remove that roadblock from the way. Finally, I will return and ask again: Is anything stopping you from succeeding now?

I do this because I want to make sure that there is no actual thing beyond their control that is stopping them. As their leader, it is my job to address any of those items and make sure that I oversee them. Once I have done so, I know the path is clear for that person to do their job without any hindrance that could interfere with them. Here is the point. Now, it is all on them. There are no outside forces or artificial barriers in their way. I mainly do this because that was probably the case all along, but I wanted to show them that I cared and was willing to do for them as they asked. Now I knew, and they knew too, that nothing was stopping them. It went like this: broken equipment? That is no problem. I will get it replaced or fixed. Not trained? That is no problem. I will ensure you get the proper training, as much as you want. What else do you need? And so on, and so on.

Is It The Facility Or You?

In most cases, it is not the facility, the equipment, or the training; it is you. For whatever reason, people seem to be afraid to confront a problem head-on and make things happen. It is like they are always waiting for someone or something else to get it done. While all along, they had the power to get things moving. Here is a real-life example. I hired a former coworker to run a shop for me. It was not the newest, prettiest, or closest shop to him. Knowing all this, I made sure that I gave him everything he wanted up front and was transparent about the shop, its challenges, and what needed to be done. How much do you want? Ok done. What else do you need? Transportation? Ok, I will give that to you, too. We did this until he had everything he wanted. This manager was a highly intelligent and capable operator who knew how to do the job. He is also likable and has an outgoing and engaging personality, which he used to his advantage in the end.

Fast forward, and he takes over the shop, and since he knows the job, things are headed in a positive direction in the beginning. Once he gets comfortable, he asks for different items to be taken care of with the facility. It's nothing crazy, and like always, I agree and approve of whatever we need to address. Now, about two months in, his requests have become a little more demanding and with a little harsher tone. Also, the shop's performance was not what I had hoped it would be with his experience level. I continued to approve whatever he wanted. Then he would complain that the repairs I approved were not good enough, so I approved whatever he wanted in addition, even though the original ones were what he asked for.

The performance continued to worsen, as did his tone and attitude. It became that nothing in the place or what I had approved of was good enough for him. He constantly complained to his team and everyone else about how bad the facility was. Yet this was the facility he knew and agreed he was going to. I also had approved and spent and overspent on everything he asked for. Mind you, I had been working with this shop for several years, and it was your typical legacy shop; nothing was wrong with it; it just didn't have all the new bells and whistles that a brand-new shop does. His main focus became the facility complaints instead of where he was falling short on the business. Then he gave an ultimatum and demanded a transfer, or else he would quit. If there is one thing that I do not believe in, it is rewarding bad behavior. Also, at this point, everyone had had enough of his negative demeanor. We stood firm; he left for a competitor, and the next manager took over and confirmed that things were not as bad as he had said. She began to fix the real problems that were created by the former manager and his attitude and perception of things. If he had just focused on his team and his mission, there would have been no problem.

The moral of this story was that the manager did not have the desire to work at that facility and see things through, nor did he have the discipline to keep his professionalism or stick to his commitment. Also, after taking him in and giving him everything he wanted, he recruited several people to work for him at his new place. Well, that is how things go sometimes, especially when people use their personality instead of their leadership traits to manage. If He had the desire to succeed, nothing would have stopped him or gotten in his way. Everything he brought up was an excuse, and as I kept taking them away from him, he just kept inflating them and making them worse. When he realized this would not work because I was willing to do whatever it took to make it right, his attitude showed its true colors, and the end was in sight. It is also a shame because this person is fully smart, talented, and capable of being a top-level manager or regional manager. However, this is the kind of thing that gets in his way. At our last job, I told him He is great when he wants to be great. The problem is that he was not when he did not want to be. Because he did not have the desire and discipline to see things through, he made a short-term decision and will continue to work at a store level, not that there is anything wrong with that. However, he has the skill and intelligence to be a multi-unit operator, not desire or discipline.

Success is in your power

Herein lies the difference in which I have always believed. That is everything was in my power to fix. I love having a can-do attitude. If I were in his shoes, I would have led the way to improve things. So many times, my family and I have come to a place I was managing and spent our weekend painting, cleaning, reorganizing, or whatever it took. I was not complaining or waiting for someone else to fix things. I was actively doing what I could with what I had to be effective. Unfortunately, most people I see do not think or do not realize this. They stop at the first bump in the road and wait for help or instructions, or I do not know what. I prefer action. Something, anything to get moving in the right direction, even if it is only a few feet. It reminds me of people stopping before a puddle and not going across. If they took the first step, they would realize that the puddle was only an inch deep and could easily cross if they had only tried. But they stand and wait instead.

Desire

This is where desire comes in. That burning constant feeling of needing to succeed and get things done. There are so many opportunities, I see because people do not take the easy, obvious steps that they should; they freeze up in front of a puddle. If more people would act and walk forward a few steps, the dividends would be tenfold, and they would be far ahead of most others. Another example, albeit differently, recently became known with a leader I work with.

There is a leader who I work with who oversees an entire state. He has been with the company longer than I have been, he has been in his position longer than I have been, and he is the presumptive nominee for the next promotion, where he would oversee several states. I presume he has a financial package commensurate with his title and tenure, including salary, bonuses, and stock options. From a distance, everything is good, and things are going fine. However, as a shock to almost everyone, he gave his notice, stepped down, and left the company. I will look at this from two sides, so bear with me, as there is a lesson to be learned here.

First, this person is successful, and no one who knows him would argue that point. Despite his hands-off approach, he is effective and well-liked inside and outside the company. The only criticism I have heard is that he is not an engaged leader but distant. However, as we are discussing, it comes down to his desire to continue progressing in his position and this company. You see, without earnest desire, you are merely going through the motions.

When you are just going through the motions, you are living a lie, not only to yourself, but everyone else sees it as well. Case in point, when someone gives their notice and has moved forward with plans to leave, I don't believe in trying to sell them and talk them out of it. Invariably, they may stay for a short time and be okay with getting more money and some other perk. However, in the long term, there is something inside of them telling them that they want something different,

Another personal example

I know how this feels because several years ago, I left the company that I had worked with for nine years. I came in as a GM, was promoted to Vice President, and collaborated directly with the owner. I thought I would never leave, and I loved the company, the owner, and what we represented. Then, things began to change somewhere around the six- or seven-year mark. The owner was going through a mid-life crisis of sorts. The man who hired me, who used to wear a business suit to work each day and conduct himself as such, began to change. It seemed like success had changed him, and his appearance and conduct also began to change. It felt like overnight; I went from working for a professional and proud company to one I compared to the Jersey Shore TV show, which was popular at the time.

I felt increasingly distanced from the owner and the company and from the direction in which things were going. I went through the motions for two years, and I can tell you that it was a horrible feeling. Each day felt like torture, and I did not have two faces; I had one, and it was evident how miserable I was working for a company and a man I did not believe in anymore. I had lost my desire to be there and to be a part of the culture that I disagreed with. I was also ostracized because I did not fit into the "cult" anymore, and the owner enjoyed playing different people against each other.

Unfortunately, what kept me there was the money and worrying about my family. Luckily, an opportunity arose that allowed me to leave that company and improve my standing instead of stepping back. I am trying to make the point that you will never succeed if you truly do not desire to work for a certain company or on a team. Without desire, it will never work out. Sadly, I look back on those final years there, and with many, what could have been. I wanted it to be what it once was and the owner to be who he once was. However, leaving was one of the best things that happened in my career, and I would not be where I am today if I had stayed. I will discuss more of this in a later chapter.

Family First

Now, getting back to my current coworker. My initial reaction was surprise and uncertainty about how he could walk away with so much on the line and potentially so much yet to come with the future he had. But do you know what? Nothing is worth two especially important things. That is your health and your family. While I have a strong desire and am very driven, I almost lost my family at that last job. The pressure, the fake culture, and the games changed who I was. I could not turn off the person I was at work with when I came home. There was no off switch to return to a caring husband and father when I was home. All day long, it was kill or be killed, and do what I want, or I will fire you and put someone else in your place.

So today, I look at my coworker's decision in a different light than I would have before. If he is making his decision based on the good of his health or his family, then he is making the right decision. I have devoted a generous portion of my life to the companies I have worked for. Again, I have had a great desire, have risen in the ranks, and have been rewarded for it. However, nothing is worth trading my family for.

Many times, my family has taken a back seat to my career. It was not on purpose, but I used to believe that by putting work first, I was putting them first. You may ask how that is possible. My thinking used to be that I might miss a game or a milestone in my kids' lives because of the greater goal of providing good things for them. An example might be that I might miss some stuff, but I am paying for their college or buying them a new car. However, as my kids have grown up and I am older, I realize how precious and priceless those moments are. It is important to provide a good life for your family, but it is also important to remember that your presents cannot replace your presence. When it is all said and done, you will not wish you worked more; you will wish you had spent more time and had more time to spend with the ones in your life who mean the most to you.

Discipline

The Ying to the yang of desire is discipline, as one is meaningless without the other. To attain any goal does not happen all at once; it happens one day and one decision at a time. It is the little steps that lead in the end to attaining the results that you desire. Just like if you want to get in shape, it takes time. There needs to be days, weeks, and months of making the right decisions, and the results will come. You cannot be frustrated the first week and quit because you do not see immediate results. You see, we are not a factory making widgets in the businesses that I have worked in my career. The auto business is full of different variables that need to be contended with. We fix cars, trucks, and SUV's. We fix Ford's, Chevy's, Honda's, Tesla's and so on. We fix cars for all the different insurance companies. We fix cars in all assorted colors. We fix cars of all different years. Finally, we fix all diverse kinds of damage, from collisions to hail, to deer, and all around and under vehicles. There is truly variability in everything we do. The only thing we can do to come out with a predictable outcome is to have the discipline to follow a process.

Process

Following a process is the only thing that you can do to smooth out some of the variables that I mentioned above so that you can predict what the outcome will be. Imagine how complicated flying a modern jet is with all the different systems and technologies. Yet, no matter how many years of experience the pilots have, they still rely on their checklists, which is how they conquer the variables. A pilot may have been flying the same plane model for 30 years, but they will still read off the checklist as if it is their first time flying. It takes discipline to do that each time they strap in the flight deck. I imagine it is true for other businesses as well, but I can tell you that when a business struggles, it can be traced back to a lack of discipline in sticking to the process. How often have you heard the term we need to return to basics? I am sure a lot, just like me. The person is saying we need to discipline ourselves to follow our process. Why did we ever stop in the first place? Because we didn't have the discipline, we needed to stick to it day in and day out.

The process brings predictability to any business. It does not matter if we are fixing cars or making pizza. If the correct process is not followed, the result will not be what you want it to be. So, if you see a business or product struggling, trace it back to a failure or misstep in the process. This way, you can treat the cause, not just the symptom. Because if you treat symptoms, you will have a lengthy line outside of your door and will be treating symptoms all day long. It sounds simple; however, humans are like herding cats sometimes, and you can quickly find yourself going off the road. Let me give you an example of why the process is needed but, without discipline, will not last long.

Lessons

My experience over thirty years has been that a business's struggles can be traced back to a lack of following its process. The reasons why a business fails to follow its process always relate to a lack of discipline in one form or another. You see, it is simple and easy to get off track when it comes to the discipline of following a process. Take, for example, a collision shop that has a process and is following it. All it takes is one day and one car when the process is not followed. Let us say one day the shop is shorthanded. Unfortunately, it is human nature to get sloppy and move on to the next task instead of slowing down and having the discipline to do the job right. Once your business breaks the process and has "dirty" vehicles in it, your ability to have a predictable outcome is compromised, and before you know it, the entire shop is compromised.

Lessons with a Mustang

For whatever reason, as humans, it is not easy to stay disciplined and do what we need to do day after day. If it were easy, our entire world would be changed for the better. To be successful, we need to force ourselves to stay disciplined. If we do, the road may take some time, but, in the end, we will be better off for it. I was reminded of this again this past weekend.

I love Foxbody Mustangs, which are an acquired taste for some people. I must really love them, as I have owned six of them. I am honored to have a good friend and true craftsman doing the bodywork on the vehicle. Rich is an A+ technician in every sense of the word, and I have the utmost respect for him and his talent. His qualifications and resume speak for themselves.

The other day, I went to the shop to watch him and lend him a hand wherever I could. His goal for the day was to seam seal the doors and hatch and plate up some holes in the firewall. It really "sounded" easy. It should not take long or be a big deal, or so I thought.

Remember, this is also an incredibly talented technician, so these minor tasks seemed like something through which he would breeze past. First up was the seam sealing. I watched him as he took great care in preparing everything, he needed to do the job. He set up the work area, the parts, the tools, and the supplies that he needed. He was in no rush and took all the time he needed to. I was impatient and wondered to myself why it was taking him so long. He then prepared the seam seal gun and nozzle. He spent time notching the nozzle so the seam seal would apply how he wanted. After checking it several times, he kept notching the nozzle until it was how he wanted. Then, to my amazement, he started to do practice passes with the applicator gun unplugged. I could not believe what I was seeing. Again, this man's reputation speaks for itself, and he is standing there doing practice runs before he applies the seam sealer. I was impressed to see his dedication and discipline for his craft. This is why he has the reputation that he does and takes steps like this.

Finally, he was ready, carefully applied the seam sealer, and then formed it wherever needed. Remember, this was not a 2024 Mercedes Benz; this was a 1992 Mustang, but his desire to be the best and his discipline to match didn't consider that. Many hours later, he started patching holes in the firewall. First, he grabbed cardboard and began drawing, forming, and cutting templates. He took his time doing this and kept going back and forth, adjusting until he had perfect cardboard templates of the needed patches. I would have expected someone with his skill to skip that step and make the metal cuts. But not a talented technician like Rich. He wanted to make them correctly, so he had the discipline not to skip this step.

Lessons from Top Gun

A few weeks ago, I held a meeting for all my General and Regional managers, and there were about forty-five people in the room. I started the meeting by playing a clip from the original Top Gun movie from 1986. As usual, there was a method behind my madness, and I was playing the clip for a leadership lesson. After Goose is killed in an accident, Maverick, played by Tom Cruise, will not engage and get into the fight. He keeps backing off instead of attacking, and Viper, played by Tom Skerritt, says keep sending him up. Many of us know the story, as finally, when the chips are down, Maverick gets engaged and helps Iceman save the day and the air battle.

I shared this in the meeting because I wanted to share a true story that applied to several of the managers in the room. We hired a well-established general manager from outside the company a few years ago. I personally knew of his experience and credentials. He worked for a company that I had in the past, and I knew of his reputation. From many different people that I trusted, I was told he was authentic and knew what he was doing. I was extremely excited to see him come on board and did not doubt that he would be a plug-and-play answer to the center that he was going to.

The manager got to the store and got his feet under him. The surprising part was that things really weren't getting any better. This made no sense; I knew he had more experience than the last manager. He had the knowledge, the experience, the training, and the pedigree, yet for some reason, nothing was changing. One day, I went to the shop to see what was happening. I saw basic mistakes being made that I knew this manager knew better than to allow. Again, I knew who he was and where he came from, and I knew that he knew what to do. I pointed them out and was sure he would handle them, so I gave it a few more weeks.

I came back again and saw the same things. Nothing had been fixed, and now I was really confused. I finally realized that it wasn't a skill issue because I knew he had skill. For some reason, it was a will issue. I sat down with him and, point by point, went over what I saw, and he agreed with each thing I said. Then it hit me: this was just like Maverick's problem in Top Gun. The hard part was done, which was finding a manager who knew what was right and what was wrong. The easy part was getting him engaged and leading his team.

I shared the Maverick analogy with him and showed him how easy it was to see what was wrong. He needed to stop holding back and now. He had the answers, and he just needed to share them. He needed to have faith in himself. I gave my manager call signs back then, so I anointed him with a call sign, Maverick. I am not saying it was this conversation, but he got engaged and quickly turned things around after it. I am not even sure why he did not do it initially, but for whatever reason, he didn't. He needed a quick reminder that he knew what he was doing and just needed to get engaged and make decisions. He went on to run that shop successfully and showed a desire and talent to become a regional manager. Unfortunately, he tragically passed away at an early age, and I never got to see him continue his growth and journey in our industry. Mike, I will forever remember you fondly, and your memory will continue to move on as it did in my meeting and on these pages. Sometimes people know what to do. They need a nudge or being believed in enough to engage and get things done.

Don't get bullied

Another movie analogy I used in this meeting unbelievably was from the beloved movie A Christmas Story. Yes, I love analogies, and as I mentioned, I look for leadership lessons everywhere. In the movie, you may remember two bullies who regularly beat up the main character, his brother, and their friends. The main bully's name was Scott Farkus, and he was immediately recognizable from the photo I put up on the screen. I shared that another pitfall to desire and discipline that I see is the manager getting bullied.

Now, of course, I don't mean that literally; I mean that, for whatever reason, leaders sometimes stand down because they are afraid to hold their team accountable. It's another example of knowing what to do as a leader but not having enough desire or discipline to make it happen. Things need to be handled as soon as they occur. An easy example is if you overhear someone in your office not speaking correctly to a customer on the phone. The right thing to do is handle the customer first and foremost. But after that, in private, it's your duty to coach that employee on what corrections they need to make next time.

However, I sometimes see managers cowering and afraid to say anything. Why? Some leaders are afraid to put themselves out there as they should, look out for their team, and help get them on the right track. I used Scott Farkus as an example because it was almost like managers are bullied and afraid to do their jobs. That's the whole reason leaders are here. To lead. If we didn't need leaders, everyone could do whatever they wanted, and there would be no standards. If you are not coaching and helping your team and know the right answers, having enough faith in yourself is a matter of speaking up. To have that faith, you need to have the desire and the discipline to educate yourself and hone your skills until you do have that faith.

Remember, no one is perfect, and you, as a leader, don't have to be perfect either. It's ok to be wrong or make mistakes. If you are humble enough to be wrong and admit it, no one will hold it against you. The problem comes when a leader is too stubborn to admit they are wrong, and they aren't open to other ways of doing things. So, if you find yourself hanging back and not engaging, push forward and remember that if you care about your team, you will show them the way. If you are still hesitating, make sure you are putting in the hard work yourself to feel the confidence you need to lead your team; after all, they are counting on you.

Never Give Up

The final story I will share with you about desire and discipline comes from a fishing trip I took with my dad. When I was twelve, our family vacationed in the Florida Keys. One of the things that we did on these trips was that my dad would charter a fishing boat, and he and I would go on a father-son fishing trip together. On this trip, I hooked a Bull Dolphin, for some reason, on a very light fishing pole. The strength and endurance of this fish was amazing, and I remember it to this day. The fight seemed to go on for hours, and each time I got the fish close to the boat, it would run much farther away.

It came to the point where I wanted to give up, and I begged my dad to take the line and help me. My arms were burning in pain, and I was exhausted. However, he kept encouraging me to keep going, and I almost had him. This went on and on, and my pain and exhaustion grew greater. I begged and pleaded with my dad, and I was surprised and hurt that he wouldn't help me, and he wouldn't take the line for me. I couldn't understand why he wouldn't help me; he was right there and easily could have taken over.

Finally, I fought through the pain, the exhaustion, and the excuses. He wasn't going to help me, and it became clear to me that no one was coming to save me. It was up to me and me alone. After what seemed like hours, I finally brought the fish in. I fished many times in my life, but that fish gave me the fight of his life. Once the fight was over, I understood what my dad did for me and the lesson he taught me that day. Yes, he easily could have taken over and handled the fish for me. I would have been able to put the rod down and rest. However, my dad wanted to teach me how to fight through adversity and not give up. He taught me how to have the desire and the discipline to succeed. Thankfully, my dad had that fish mounted, and I still have it to this day. Thirty-five years later, the lesson of not giving up and fighting through still holds true to this day.

As a leader of leaders it's important to show the way and sometimes go it alone if you believe that what you are doing is right. This takes desire and discipline which are two traits that you can learn and put into practice. Without them, even the strongest of beliefs and visions will fail. Desire and discipline are what makes things stick and what gets you to the finish line when the going gets tough or people are pushing back against you for whatever reason.

The Extra Mile

1. Remove people's roadblocks
2. Success is in your power
3. Have the desire to get things done
4. Family First
5. Stick to the process
6. Get Engaged
7. Don't be bullied
8. Never give up

PATIENCE

Let's talk about the importance of patience in a multi shop or multi business leadership role. For my entire career I would characterize myself as an aggressive leader, and proudly so. On the front-line level, there usually isn't a lot of time for patience as you need to constantly get things done in real time, and I was able to do this very effectively. As you move from store level to regional level and higher, learning and practicing patience takes on more importance. At these higher levels, things don't happen as fast, and you aren't expected to just rush in and force things to happen in this kind of role. However, my current book of business is diverse and includes different kinds of businesses as well. Currently I lead collision businesses, scanning and calibration businesses, glass businesses, as well as mechanical businesses. Having this diversity of types of businesses calls for patience as you cannot have the same focus on each as they are all different and call for a different strategy.

I have found myself purposely having to focus my train of thought on each one individually and separately to reset my thinking and my strategy. At a General Manager level, you are leading your troops, and there is a certain skillset in getting things done. In moving up to Regional or District Manager, now you are a leader of leaders, and this takes a different skillset. In a Regional Vice President role, you are now leading Regional Managers. This too takes on a new dynamic that requires more growth on your part. I was recently asked to host a call on patience and how it impacts results.

When I sat down to prepare my thoughts about patience, I began to think about what visuals I could use that would remind me of patience in everyday life and would be easy to understand and relate to. I like looking for leadership examples everywhere I can and in everyday life. In preparing for this call on patience, here are a few quick examples that you may be able to relate to that can be tied into patience.

The Pizza Lesson

I enjoy cooking and baking as a hobby, and recently I've been making homemade dough for baking my own pizza and bread at home. If you have ever tried to do this yourself, you will know that there is no way to rush the process of making homemade dough from scratch. The simple ingredients need time to work together. Also, the yeast takes its time to do its work and even in our world of 2024 it cannot be rushed or sped up just like it couldn't be two thousand years ago. Even once the ingredients are mixed, there is no way to rush the process of fermentation. To properly prepare dough to make pizza you need to start the day before and prepare for the next day's product. If you are impatient, you aren't going to be able to make pizza from scratch. You will get something, but it won't be delicious pizza.

Even when the process is happening, you may not see anything and think that it's not working. This weekend I made Focaccia bread from scratch and the process took ten hours from when I started to when there was something to eat. Most of the time was spent with me doing nothing and the yeast doing everything. As I waited, I thought of how this relates to business too. As a Regional Vice President, I am only one person, and I cannot get the immediate course corrections in place and moving and as fast as I would have at other levels of leadership. If I stood watching the mixture, many times I would have been convinced that nothing was happening. However, by going away and giving it time, and coming back, I was able to see the progress. So fresh pizza or bread dough was the first thing that I thought of in making the connection that certain things take time and there is no way to make them happen faster, as well as at times looking like nothing was happening. An exercise like making homemade dough is a lesson in learning patience.

The Fishing Lesson

Then I turned to something I did a lot of with my father when I was younger, that is fishing. For those of us who have gone fishing in our lives, that may be the ultimate lesson in patience. When you are fishing, you spend most of your time preparing and waiting, not actually with a fish on the line. Think of it this way, with fishing there is planning time, prepping time, waiting time, then finally the result. The plan might be let's go fishing Sunday at six in the morning at the lake. The preparation might include choice of rods, lures, and bait. The action of putting your line in the water only takes seconds, and then you wait.

Most of my memories are of those times just on the water with my father. I think of times spent together talking and just enjoying each other's company. I don't really remember if we caught anything or not. That is what patient fishing is like. It's not about the rush for fish or we could also say results. It's more about the process, the time spent and the comradery. If you are impatient when you are fishing, it's not a fun day at all. Pull the lines up, put the lines down. Move the boat from here, to here, to here. Change baits over and over. Those kinds of days on the water are anything but fun and I've had those days too. Since we can't see the results below the water, our impatience may be costing us results. What if the area is good and the fish were just noticing your bait and getting ready to try it. But before they can strike, you pull everything up and move. Fishing takes time and patience to see things through. It's a great example to remember in business. How many times do we change directions before the fruits of our actions begin showing up. If you have taken the time to prepare and have put things into action that should bring good results, make sure you are giving it enough time to work.

Lessons in fiction

Next, I thought of two movies characters that are each the opposites of patience. In the famous movie The Godfather. Sonny Corleone played by James Caan, and Michael Corleone played by Al Pacino, certainly can be shown as opposite examples of patience, and even here there is a lesson to be learned. If you have ever seen the movie, you know that Sonny is a hothead fueled by his emotions. While Michael is slow, cold, calculating, and strategic. Sonny has no patience, and he reacts as his emotions take him in whatever direction. His story ultimately ends with his murder because he couldn't see what was happening through the fog of his anger.

Whereas Michael shows great patience in waiting for situations to come his way and takes his time to maneuver until he is in a stronger position, ready to make his move. I've used these two-character examples several times in the past. If I have someone angry and fueled with emotion that I am working with, I've often told them to be less Sonny and more Michael. Of course, this is an extreme example, and I use it for effect here. The correlation is easy to see for business. It's better to be detached from your emotions and to see things in a calm and patient manner as opposed to allowing your emotions to carry you in whatever direction they may take you. I've seen managers in the past that constantly fly off the handle when any little things don't go their way.

Right now, I have a particular manager in my head who was actually very knowledgeable and talented in running a collision shop. However, he may be the most angry and emotional person I've ever met. He would argue with just about anyone over just about anything. It didn't matter how minor the issue; he would take it way too far and fight to win the most inconsequential issue. He managed to anger insurance partners, customers, teammates, and his own management chain because he was unable to calm his emotions and not be led by them. Each week I would spend time apologizing to a variety of people for his actions. No matter how small the matter was he wanted to "win." Not every topic is important, especially if you win a pyrrhic victory. As I said, the shame of this was that his knowledge was there, and he was very talented at his job. Unfortunately, though he refused to control himself and the baggage he brought overcame his good points and few people wanted to work with him. He ultimately left the company and of course blamed everyone but himself.

Lessons in History

As I mentioned earlier, I am a student of military history, immediately another example came into my mind. Both General George S. Patton and General Dwight D. Eisenhower were famous American Generals from World War Two, and they both helped America win the war. However, how they went about their successes were both completely different. General Patton was a fiery, aggressive, break glass in case of emergency kind of commander. When you needed immediate help or solutions in an impossible situation, you turned to Patton. His record shows time and time again his ability to help where the odds were stacked against him. His impact was sudden, violent, and effective.

One of the dichotomies of General Patton was that he rubbed some people the wrong way and his aggressiveness could be used against him. As Karl Malden said in the 1970 movie Patton as he played General Omar Bradley, "George, you can be a pain in the neck." So, for all his success, his career was plagued by his temper, rashness, and lack of patience. He was even relieved of his command in the Sicily campaign for losing his temper and slapping two American soldiers. Even after performing brilliantly in his dash across France and Germany in speeding the European war to an end, his temperament cost him once again. Because of his reluctance to obey the commands of his superiors and fears he would ignite a war with the Soviets, he was again placed on the sidelines. For all his success and achievements, his inability to show restraint and patience cost him his career.

On the contrary, General Eisenhower was tasked with the administration, planning, and team building of the entire Allied effort in winning the war in Europe. The fate of millions of people depended on Eisenhower's ability to keep the Allied team together and working toward their common goal. Eisenhower showed great patience in ways that Patton wouldn't have ever been able to. Eisenhower directed and led the invasions of North Africa, Sicily, and Normandy. Not only were the final outcomes successful but he was also able to keep the Allied team fighting together as opposed to fighting each other.

Eisenhower was able to see his mission through and then also become elected President and lead the United States into the Cold War. It's easy to look back and see how successful it all was. But if you go back and study things as they happened it's a different story. Eisenhower had to contend with several different personalities with different languages and different goals. Not only that but people also wanted to further their own personal or national goals ahead of the main goal of freeing Europe from tyranny. Eisenhower never commanded an army in the field, but he accomplished a greater goal in keeping the Allied countries together and working for their common good instead of against each other. This put a great emotional and personal strain on Eisenhower, and he was known to smoke countless cigarettes and drink gallons of coffee. However, through great patience and keeping his emotions in check, General Eisenhower was a huge success and the world to this day owes him a debt of gratitude.

Earlier in my career I would have compared myself and been thrilled to do so as having more of a Patton style. If you needed something done or some goal accomplished, I was your guy. I was able to be a "problem" solver, and you could send me into any situation and I could get it "fixed." The problem was, much like Patton, I didn't care about the people part of the scenario.

Early in my career, people we more of a nuisance to the "important" part of fixing the situation. Hard lessons taught me that this wasn't the right answer and that was not the leader or the man that I wanted to be. Today, I have grown into a different kind of leader than the Patton model. I still value being an aggressive leader as that sets you apart from many in the field of leaders, but I no longer push it to the Patton level of success at all costs. If anything, I would like to be more like an aggressive Eisenhower. I wish there was a better word for me to use than aggressive.

Even the word can tend to be misunderstood, as I learned recently. I was participating in helping lead a class recently. The leader of the class asked us to find an adjective that starts with the first letter of our first name. Immediately I picked Aggressive Angelo with pride. Unfortunately, she didn't like that at all and felt that was a negative. It's a shame that being an aggressive leader would be looked upon as a negative. That certainly wasn't my goal though. My goal was to show that I have a get it done kind of sprit. We both saw the side of the other though and I offered Authentic Angelo instead and we used both in the end, because both are true for me.

There was another example that I used for the presentation on patience that this one may be the most outlandish of all, but it hits close to home for me. The final example I used between the two sides of patience was Yoda and Darth Vader from the movie franchise Star Wars. Most of us know how the story goes, Yoda stands for everything good, and Vader stands for everything bad. They both get results, but they go about it in completely different ways. Yoda is patient, humble and wants to help others. Vader is cold, cunning, ruthless, and self-centered.

Again, I think of the way I used to do things and yes, I got results. I was also a product of the place I was working for at the time where it was kill or be killed. The owner only cared about his own pocket and pitted everyone against each other, and I became very good at being Darth Vader. One of the many problems with this model is that it not only takes a toll on you but also takes a toll on those around you. I wasn't a fun person to be around or to work with. I was a machine just looking for results and to get things done. Not only that but it was a constant feeling of pressure that I shared not only with my work team but also my family at home.

Beware of working in toxic work environments like this. Not every day can be an emergency. If at where you work, every day is an emergency, then you are in a toxic environment. This isn't healthy, and work should not be the be all end all in your life. This mentality that I had also had a detrimental effect on my family too. Again, each day was a pressure cooker, and I wasn't good at shutting it off. It was just always there. I lived it during the day, and I brought it home at night. I barked orders to get things done at work so why wouldn't I do that at home too. It wasn't a pretty picture, and I am thankful that I didn't lose my family because of it. No job is worth losing the ones that mean most to you in life. It's not always easy to identify though when you are stuck in the middle of it. Only after I left that organization was I able to start seeing how toxic it was and the effect that it had on me. It was after I had gone that people started telling me how different I was and what positive changes I had gone through.

Beware of Haste and Emotion

Each example can be brought back with some license to daily business and what we do in our careers. Patience in decision making is the longer but more sustainable road. Patience gives us the time to consider the bigger picture, not just quick decisions for quick results. This thought process has come in handy for me when I make decisions in the current businesses that I am responsible for. I currently am responsible for business names that are national brands that go from coast to coast. I am sobered by the thought that the decisions that I make could have an impact on people and shops that I don't directly lead at all. If I make decisions based on emotion and not patience, people can lose their jobs and not be able to feed their families because of me.

Remember our decisions are like the ripples created when a stone is thrown into a pond. With patience, I remember to look at the big picture and carefully consider the options I have before me and the potential outcomes they bring. Patience allows us to think for the entire good of the organization and the future of the organization. I want the decisions that I am making today to stand the test of time beyond when I have hung it up and called it a career. I also want them to stand up for the next generation of teammates and leaders that will come after me. This really hits close to home for me as my wife and my two sons work in this industry as well and I want them to not only be proud to work in it but also be proud of the work I did as a leader.

Decisions based on emotion are the opposite of patient decisions. If you are not patient, you may change course before things have a chance to grow. Another analogy is that of a seed which was planted and has been tended to and watered by the farmer. However, the sprout had not broken the plane of the soil yet, so it looks like nothing is happening. Like this sprout, changes and progress are happening sometimes beneath the surface and you just can't see the results yet. If you act impatiently, you may scrap that plan which was just about to show its fruits and start over, destroying the progress which was about to show and had already been accomplished. Fight the urge to jump from decision to decision without patiently and carefully considering them. Being impatient with your team can also deflate them and their desire to work with you. We have all heard the term "flavor of the month" before. No team gets excited when they feel something is just a flavor of the month topic. Why get engaged or put the work into something where everyone feels that it will just come to go to something else next month?

Resist the urge to jump from that metric or that as that becomes flavor of the month. You can't change ten things at a time. Focus on one or two core goals at a time and then be disciplined to follow through with them. It takes time to turn an aircraft carrier into the wind to launch an aircraft. In business too, it takes time for a team to focus and change their way of doing things. Then it takes time for that way of doing business to take root and show the results. Tactics may move quickly but your strategy should not. This is where something I call the "Leadership Comma" comes in for me.

Use the Leadership Comma

"Leadership Comma" is the term that I coined for the short pause in between my emotions and my decision making. In the past, I allowed my emotions to fuel my decisions. This would be the opposite of patience. Something would happen, i.e., a trigger, and then without consideration, my emotions would take over and I would come to regret my actions and words. As we all know, once you say or do something you regret there is no going back. You may say you are sorry or seek forgiveness, but you can never take those words or actions back as if they never happened. These unbridled emotions have hurt me more than once in my life and in my career.

Most times when I made these mistakes, only shortly thereafter did I realize my regret and my mistake. If only there was a way to delay making decisions based on emotion. There is, but you must invoke it, it's called the Leadership Comma. It's very simple when you keep it at the forefront of your mind. When there is a trigger and you begin to get emotional, take two steps. The first is to acknowledge the emotion and the second is to pause without making any decision or reaction. For me, my reaction was anger to most triggers. Here is an example; I get word that something I was expecting isn't going to happen like I thought. It could be a shop that said they would make their budget yesterday, and now is going to miss by a wide margin. I still will feel that emotional reaction of anger rising. However now I acknowledge the emotion first. It looks like this, "ok, I feel I am getting angry because the store is going to miss plan." Now that I acknowledge the anger, I remember that it doesn't control my reactions, it's just there. Next, I Pause in some way. I might take a walk, I might grab a cup of coffee, anything.

The important point is that I allow time for my emotions to cool. Before I might have called someone or fired off an email before I had a chance to think things through. What tended to happen was that my emotional response was worse than the actual situation, but that's what was remembered, me and my bad response. Of course, then I was left with paying the price of not being able to control my emotions. I used to say that I was like a hockey player who had been cross checked in the back, but nobody saw that. They only saw my reaction of slashing the guy in the back of the legs in return. However, only I ever went in the penalty box.

That is how the Leadership Comma works for me, trigger, acknowledge, pause, decide. This has allowed me the time and patience to consider decisions before just reacting to them. When I reacted to things, I allowed my emotions to steer me into places that I didn't want to go. I hope that sharing this with you helps to do the same for you. Remember your decisions and actions will most likely outlive your time in whatever position you are in. When you allow your emotions to get the better of your intelligence, it's never a good thing. When you're emotional, it may make sense in your own head, but it can't in anyone else's. It's an eye-opening opportunity when you're able to keep your emotions under control while you watch and don't react to someone who can't. It's hard because when you're in the heat of the moment you can't see it. However, when you can stay calm, it's like watching a child throw a temper tantrum. The fun part is when you can't keep your cool and watch and laugh inside at how ridiculous it looks.

Too Much Patience?

I was asked a question the other day that brings up a good point. The question was, "it is possible to have too much patience?" I answered by asking a question back, "is it possible to drink too much water?" Of course, the answer is yes. I countered with, "but water is good for you." My comparison is obvious, even water which is good for you can be bad if you use it in excess. So, my answer is yes, there is such a thing as too much patience. You can wait too long without doing anything or taking any action. At that point you aren't a leader, you are just existing, you aren't doing anything.

In all the examples in the beginning of the chapter, there comes a time where decisions need to be made, and changes are in order. For example, if you waited more than enough time, and the dough isn't rising, it's possible the yeast went bad, and it will never rise. If you wait too long you will have nothing to eat, whereas if you throw it away and start over, you may still have enough time to enjoy pizza. The goal is to make sure that you have waited enough time but not too much time. I have seen leaders who haven't made a change in years. Same people, same processes, same results. My question is why are you even here then? If you don't ever change anything, things would be the same if you weren't even here. As a leader you are here to make an impact. You are here to help, coach, and train your team to success. Keeping to the status quo isn't doing anything for anyone and that isn't what being a leader is about.

Things aren't always going to go according to plan, that is just a simple fact of life. There are times when you feel that you did everything right and for some reason things don't turn out that way you wanted them to. A natural reaction may be to run in and get things moving. Makes changes, kick some butt, or whatever may have worked for you in the past. In my current position I am learning the art of patience more than ever. With the bigger picture that I am responsible for, sometimes change and progress doesn't happen as quickly as I would like, or I am used to.

At first it wasn't natural for me to keep waiting when things didn't turn right around. However, I kept double checking what we were doing and the people we had in place, and I confirmed in my mind that what we were doing was right, even if the metrics and results didn't tell us so just yet. A few subpar months went by, and it took everything I had not to grab the wheel and make course corrections. I had faith in my managers, and what they were doing, and I kept my hands off, even though it wasn't easy. I'm glad I did because if I did that, I would have shown a total lack of faith in my team and the hard work that they were doing. By standing back and showing faith in them, I allowed the work they were putting in to show the fruit of change and the results turned around.

As the leader, you don't always have to be the calvary riding to the rescue. You should pretty much never be, not in these higher-level roles. My goal today is to be in the background not the foreground. My goal is to help, coach, teach, train, and mentor other leaders. What good is it if everyone knows that I am just going to push in front of them and fix everything and take the credit? How deflating would that be to my team. The key lesson I have learned is that by doing less personally but by leading and nurturing my team, I can accomplish so much more and so can they. I gain success not by my own hands, but by theirs., and by their teams.

Remember the first question that you are asked in an interview for a promotion. That is "who is going to take your place?" So, if you are the doer, who did you prepare for the next level if you are everywhere doing everything? The answer is no one, it's not about you. As a good leader you should always be preparing everyone for their next levels so that you can quickly and proudly stand aside, and your team is ready to carry things forward without you. My goal is to be the least important person in my group. Thinking of it from that perspective, patience takes on even more importance. Patience truly is an art and a virtue, and you can't have too little or too much, you need just the right amount.

The Extra Mile

1. Homemade Pizza doesn't care about your timeline.
2. The Fish don't want to get caught.
3. Michael or Sonny? Lessons in Fiction.
4. Eisenhower or Patton? Lessons in History.
5. Beware of Haste and Emotion.
6. Use the Leadership Comma.
7. Pitfalls of too much patience.

THE PRESENCE OF A LEADER

Many times, in the past I have contemplated what it means to have a leader's presence. What does a leader look like? Sound like? Walk like? Talk like? I certainly know the first thought that came to my mind when that question was first posed to me many years ago. Again, being a student of military history, the first people that enter my mind are Generals and Admirals. As I ponder that question, the scowls of General Patton and Admiral Halsey enter my mind.

While it may be the first thing that I used to think of, it is certainly not all there is to the story. As I have learned, and as I have thought and grown as a leader myself, my feelings have changed. There are so many more facets that a leader can and should have more than just their initial appearance and a tough-looking scowl on their face. As a matter of fact, when you peel back the layers of leadership there is so much more to a leader than that. Mother Theresa was a leader and I'm sure she had a leader's presence, but she certainly didn't have an angry scowl. Ronald Reagan certainly had a leader's presence as well and yet he disarmed people with his smile and humor. I'm sure that there are many more examples that you can think of in your own head too.

Whenever I'm hosting a meeting that calls for an icebreaker question, I always like to ask the participants who the most famous person is they have ever actually met. For me, there is only one answer, and I remember it like it was yesterday. I visited the annual World War Two Weekend in Reading Pennsylvania many years ago. This event is a large airshow and celebration of everything from the World War Two era. Part of the event was being able to meet veterans from World War Two, shake their hands, have a chat, or get their book signed. This particular year, General Paul Tibbets would be there signing his book. If you think you never heard of him, maybe you recognize the title of his book, "Return of the Enola Gay."

General Tibbets oversaw the 509th Composite Group and Operation Silverplate charged with delivering America's new atomic bomb weapons to actual targets in war. He was behind the controls of the B-29 Enola Gay that dropped the atomic bomb on Hiroshima Japan on August 6th, 1945. Being a student of military history, I had studied the career of General Tibbets at length. During the war, Tibbetts was just a Light Colonel in his late twenties and had the power of the Commander in Chief, the President of the United States behind him. No request Tibbett's made could be turned down if he used the special codename Silverplate.

Only two men in history can say they dropped an atomic bomb in war, only one can say they planned and led the entire operation. So, when I approached the table, I knew the things that this man accomplished in his life and the times and people that he dealt with. I saw before me a man white with age, but his presence still spoke for itself. Even though his hair was white, and he was wearing hearing aids, he still had a presence that could not be missed. As I approached him, he looked me in the eyes as I greeted him. Then he turned to the mission at hand and signed a copy of his book for me. He stretched out his hand for me to shake as he handed the book back to me and I said, "Thank you, General." I knew that I was in the presence of a great leader even though his historic deeds were long in the past.

That moment so many years ago still stands clear for me. I shook the very hand that was flying the controls of that famous B-29 Super Fortress in August of 1945. I shook the hand of a man who met presidents and high-ranking military leaders. I saw a man whose personal actions helped to end World War Two The eyes that looked at me saw more in his lifetime than I will probably ever see. While old and gray, he was still the man who saw and did all those things, and it was evident in the way he carried himself and the way people reacted to him. A major historical figure like General Tibbets is an extreme example. I don't suspect that in our daily life as leaders, we will be expected to have the leadership presence that General Tibbets had, but I do think having a leadership presence is important. I will explore some of the things that I believe go into having a leader's presence. Here's the great part, it costs you virtually nothing other than being aware to set yourself ahead of so many others who do not take the time for these basics.

Timeliness

Before you ever are seen or speak, the most important thing you can do is be on time. When I say be on time, I abide by the adage that you may have heard before. "To be early is to be on time, to be on time is to be late, to be late is to be forgotten." I can't stress enough how important your timeliness is. Is shows many things to whoever you are meeting, whether that is in person or online or even calling. If you say you will arrive or call at a certain time, it is a small promise or commitment. If you come through it builds trust that if you can be trusted with small things, then maybe you can be trusted with big things too. However, if you prove that by being late you cannot hold to these small commitments then it has the opposite effect.

With all the technology today available to us, is there any acceptable reason for being late for anything other than you just didn't care? You can set alarms, and check weather and traffic from your phone. You can do those things from days before so that if traffic is taking longer than expected you can see it from days before. Are you flying to a meeting? You can check how long your flight takes or the weather in the city you are going to. By taking the time to do this extra mile of work you are showing people that if you go out of your way for minor things like this, that you will do the same or more for big things.

This counts for online meetings too. If you set a start time for a Microsoft Teams call to start at 10 am. Then you need to start the meeting at 10 am. It is frustrating to be on time for a scheduled call and the host waits until 10:05 am for late stragglers. That shows no appreciation for the people who were early and on time. So, if you say a meeting starts at 10 am make sure you are ready and set up at the latest at 9:55 am and start the meeting promptly as the clock strikes 10 am.

When you show up late to any kind of meeting you show disrespect for the other person's time. It is extremely frustrating to be early or on time for something and be forced to sit and wait for someone who cannot hold themselves accountable to do the same. When someone is late, before I ever see them or hear them, I have already judged them as someone who potentially can't be trusted with whatever they are meeting me about. It has already set things off on the wrong footing.

There are no excuses. I have often left extremely early for a meeting just to be safe. That way if something unexpected happens, I still have time built into my schedule for it. I may have gotten into a traffic jam or gotten lost, but the person I was meeting with never knew because I was still early. What's the harm in getting to the meeting location or area early? At least you are there. Now you can find a coffee shop or restaurant in the area or just sit in the parking lot and catch up on emails. At least now you know that you won't be delayed and can walk into the building fifteen minutes before your scheduled time.

Appearance

In business, it is expected that certain people will present themselves in certain ways. For instance, if you are meeting with an officiant for your wedding, chances are you will not expect them to be wearing shorts and a ripped Motley Crue tee shirt. Now there is nothing wrong with that but it's just not what you are expecting, and it may make you question their qualifications.

There are many more examples that I can use, but I think you get the point. Your appearance typically needs to fit the level that you have achieved in your career. Whether it's fair or unfair, a businessperson or a manager is expected to carry and present themselves in a certain way that coincides with the duties of the position that they have. The way that you carry and present yourself shows both respect for your position and your teammates and customers. If you can't handle responsibility for the way you look, how can you take responsibility for businesses and your employees?

Your appearance is the first thing that people will see and judge you for even before you open your mouth. You are certainly your brand and to present that brand well starts with a proper appearance. Take the extra time to care for your appearance and it will speak volumes for the skills you have and who you are as a person. I have had the honor of sitting on many panel interviews and more often than you think, candidates have set the wrong tone for when they walk in too casually dressed. You have heard it said that you should not dress for the job that you have but for the job that you want, and I believe that to be true. If you find yourself in an interview there is no harm in "overdoing" it by wearing a suit or a dress. It shows that you have taken the time and have respect for the position of the interviewers and yourself. Believe it or not,

I make it a point to see if I can tell if the person took the time to button the small button on the arm of a dress shirt. You know the one, it's not easy to get and a lot of people skip it. I always look to see if the people took the time to struggle with that small button. Unfortunately, too often people skip it and take the easy road. When I see that I also wonder what else they take the easy road on. Will they do the same in their job responsibilities? So always take the time to present yourself with care. It's easy and it goes a long way.

Speech

Another important part of having a good leadership presence is the way that you speak. Different circumstances call for different styles of speech. If I have a meeting with the C-Suite, I will take care that my words and speech are proper for that occasion. If I am out having a beer with the guys, I may be a little looser. However, when you attain higher positions in your career it becomes more important to always speak properly, second most to your appearance.

I'll give you an example, there are times when I would purposely allow my language to get a little saltier as I felt that it helped to make the point that I was trying to make. Maybe that was a little bit of General Patton's influence. However, after one such meeting, I was pulled aside by a mentor that I have a lot of respect both personally and professionally. First, I was glad that she had the guts to tell me what she had on her mind as I know it wasn't easy. She explained to me that leaders needed to hold themselves to a higher standard and that by using foul language I was not accomplishing that goal.

You see, as a high-caliber leader it was not acceptable for me to sprinkle in that language anymore, I needed to be better than that, to hold myself to a higher standard than that. That conversation has stuck in my mind so strongly and I am so thankful that she cared enough about me to talk to me about it. To this day if I feel tempted to use an off-color word, I remember that day and I smile and don't allow myself to take that easy road.

Again, it's not for me to judge but a person with a true leader's presence doesn't need to use foul language to get their point across, it only brings them down. Just like if you met the governor of your state, you expect to see them dressed properly, you would also expect them to speak properly too. So far, we know nothing about your skills. Yet if you dress properly and speak properly, you've already put yourself ahead of many others who may have better qualifications than you.

Calmness

As you rise in the ranks you will be faced with new and different challenges. Some of these may be matter of fact, while others can be downright scary. As a leader, you must train yourself not to overreact and restrain your emotions. Things are never as good as they seem or as bad as they seem. If I am having a day where everything is going right and I am the hero, I don't allow myself to get too excited about it. Why? Because many times on the very next day nothing would go right, and I was the zero.

Which one was right? Probably neither but if I allowed myself to get too high on the totem pole only to crash through the basement the next day is like riding on a roller coaster which no one wants.

So, when things are going well, I take it in stride and be thankful for it. Just the same when they aren't I remember the proverb "This too shall pass." It's not fun working with someone whose emotions are out of control. I have worked with people like that in the past. Not every moment or every day can be an emergency, nor should it. Being emotional takes a toll on people. No matter what happens, take it in stride and be calm. Don't allow your emotions to dictate your actions, as most often they will lead you down a bad road. Instead, allow yourself the time to contemplate the situation and what should be done. Many times, you don't need to immediately spit out an answer. That is unless of course there is a situation where someone's safety is at risk. But short of that, there is time for you to think of a solution.

I recall a court proceeding that I needed to go to for an accident when I was younger. I was trying to answer the other attorney's questions so fast it was tripping me up. My lawyer pulled me aside and said let him ask his question completely, pause, then give me a chance to speak first if I need to. That was great advice. Just settle down, be calm, listen to the entire question, and then pause before you answer. You can use the same tactic with situations. Don't react until you have a full picture of what is going on and then pause as you consider the potential solutions. Once you have the chance to do that, then offer the best solution you can. Again, unless it's someone's safety there is no reward for speaking or coming up with the answer first.

I'm also a sucker for good movie analogies. In the movie Hellcats of the Navy with Ronald Reagan, there are some great leadership lessons. In that movie, Reagan was the submarine Captain and must contend with his emotional executive officer, and they continually clash. In the crucial moment of the movie, Reagan is diving to try to untangle a cable in the submarine's propeller, and his executive officer is in temporary command. Finally, the other officer is faced with being in charge himself and having to make life-and-death decisions and it's not as easy as it seemed before. As Reagan gets tangled in the cable there is a report of a Japanese destroyer approaching. Reagan orders him to dive the submarine to save it and the rest of the crew even if it means that he will die. The officer was not used to making decisions like this and furiously told the captain that we wouldn't leave him and began ordering other divers into the water to help the captain. Reagan calmly reminds him that there are eighty-one men aboard that submarine and that they are the executive officer's responsibility.

That scene sends chills up my spine because it's the crux of what being a leader is all about. It's about taking care of your people first and foremost. Their needs come before your needs. Their needs may even come before the needs of the company. A good leader, if they accomplish nothing else, makes sure that his or her people are taken care of and have what they need to get their job properly done. I take more pride in the teams that I lead approving of me as their leader than of those above me on how they would judge me. These are the people who are looking to you daily for answers and know that you are guiding them to the right place. So, when I think of who my responsibility is to, I don't only think of the over three hundred reports I have under my hierarchy, I think about their families as well. My decisions can affect so many, that it is sobering to think of, and it should be.

Heart

A real leader cares about the people he or she works with and wants to see them succeed. A real leader is bothered by what bothers his or her team. We aren't robots and unless you are a cold uncaring person, and I have met plenty of those, your team does become like a second family. I wouldn't be the leader that I am without my heart. Now it has also cost me at times, but I view my heart as a strength not as a weakness. Most leaders that I have worked with in the past only cared about themselves, their pockets or their promotions. It is something I still don't understand, how some of the people that I worked for got their position. If it comes down to choosing between themselves and their team, they will pick themselves.

Early in my career, I never heard of the term servant leader which so many of us know today but once again I had an early example of that, even if I didn't know what it was called. When I was growing up, I remember my father always buying everyone a Thanksgiving turkey for Thanksgiving that worked for him. I have many examples that I remember but this is one of the ones that stand out. My dad wanted to make sure that his employees and their families had a turkey on their table, and he made sure they did. In today's fast-paced large-scale world, it is easy to lose sight of a small act of kindness like that. It's a piece of what I feel we are missing today, just having a heart, and caring for others. Others may indeed be smarter than me and may go farther than me. However, I would never trade their position if I had to give up my heart and how much I care for people.

There is a dichotomy with that thought that you need to be aware of and watch out for. That is that most people don't feel the same way and it's not reciprocal. If you realize that going into the situation and accept that you will be okay. If you think and expect that people will have the same heart and show you the same kindness, unfortunately, you will be sadly disappointed. We humans tend to grade ourselves on the curve will we grade others on a straight line. When we fall short of the expectation, we come up with excuses for why. Unfortunately, when it's the other party that falls short, there are no excuses allowed.

So, it's good to have a heart and it's even better to not expect anything in return. That way you will be wonderfully surprised and appreciative when someone does show you the same care and heart. I never let that thought stop me when I am caring and doing something for someone else. I believe that when you have been given a gift, it is your duty to share that gift. There have been many that I have given my blood, sweat, and tears to someone and they left and went to someone else for a little more money or whatever the situation may be. I've opened my home to people and treated them like family only for them to turn their back on me. That's okay, I don't regret anything I did for anyone and will do the same again tomorrow. Having a heart is a strength. Never let business become more important than being a caring human to people.

Lead from the front!

One of the tough things that happens when you get promoted is you can easily lose your touch and feel for the front lines of the business. I see it everywhere I look in today's business, especially when you spend so much time in meetings whether virtual or live, or on calls. Everything seems easy when you are in a meeting room. It becomes hard to understand why "they" just can't listen and do what they are told.

However, if you get out of your office and over to the front lines the answer is easy. I see this at my level and I'm sure it's true everywhere. Higher-ups want to give you their answers, but they don't want to ask you what you truly need, and it's very frustrating. Technology is great, meetings and calls are good tools, Microsoft Teams and Excel are great technology, but they can only give you an idea that something is wrong. To get the answers, you need to get out of the office and away from all of that to get down to the floor level.

Get out into the front lines, look, listen, and observe. Most importantly, ask the team out on the floor how things are going and what they think they need. Most times they are more than happy to tell you exactly what is wrong and exactly is needed. If you don't ask, or if you aren't there to be seen, you will never get the right answers. Sometimes you just need to bring the team together to talk. It's ok to be open and allow there to be a forum where everyone comes together and shares how they feel. Some people won't share how they feel until you pull it out of them and give them a safe place to share their opinions and how they truly feel.

When I was charged with running one location, I could see and hear everything that went on and it was easy to coach and guide things as they happened on the spot. I loved working with the same people every day and talking to them or eating lunch and enjoying a cup of coffee with them. These were the people that I saw each day and I enjoyed that time spent with them very much. Then when I became a regional manager and I was responsible for eight stores, it became much harder to keep that feeling. Somehow, I was a part of each of those teams but at the same time, I was a part of none of those teams. Part of me had to give up that tight connection, for a different kind of connection. You see each team now depended on me differently.

Fast forward to being responsible for thirty-nine separate locations and several mobile businesses. Again, I had to adapt to a different way of life, and yet still be there for everyone. However, I can't be right there and see and hear everything like I used to. That's something a leader must contend with and realize that things aren't as simple to understand as they once were. It's part of the job, no one means to become detached from the front lines, it just happens this way. My days are filled with responsibilities that come with the job that I am currently doing, just like everyone else. My job is no more important or less important than anyone else's, it's just different. I need to guard against rashness, as things may not be what they used to be. So, if something isn't going right, or it's going too right, a walk out to the front lines may be in order. You can gain so much information and perspective by just asking and talking to the front-line team. They most often know exactly what they need, they just wish someone would ask.

Preparation

I was never in the Boy Scouts. But if there is one thing that I have always worked hard on, it's being prepared. Even if I was a kid and helping my dad with some project, I tried to be prepared for whatever he needed next. I may not be the smartest guy out there. However, I will beat you by outworking you and being more prepared. You see when I was younger in grad school and high school, I didn't care. There were kids smarter than me, and I thought that was that. I didn't work hard, I didn't apply myself, and I didn't put the extra mile work in. I never cared enough to do more, and it showed. Thankfully for me, something clicked after high school, and it was easy to see. I applied to three colleges and guess what, all three of them said? No thank you, your grades aren't good enough to get in.

That was certainly a wakeup call for me and I didn't like the feeling of rejection at all. My dad used to say when I was younger that he wanted me to go to The Wharton School of Business at Penn and I didn't even know what that was. Here I was and I was told no from Saint Joseph's University, Rutgers University, and Rowan University. This rejection was one of the greatest things to happen in my life. This led me to the two-year County school. When I first got there, I heard a professor say we aren't going to come looking for you, you are expected to show up, if you don't you will fail and that's that. For the first time in my life, it was up to me, and no one was going to force me to do anything.

For whatever reason, something finally clicked, and I realized that it was up to me, and no one was going to come after me or save me. I also didn't like that feeling of rejection and not being wanted. Finally, I realized that the key was hard work and preparation. I knew for the first time that my time in class wasn't enough, and I had to put in as much time or more outside of school to make it happen. Again, the answer seemed so easy once I got it, but before that I never considered it. In the four semesters that it took to get my associate degree, I made the Dean's list for having good grades. I was used to being on the Dean's list in high school, but this time it wasn't the Dean of Discipline. I then applied again to Rowan and Rutger's and was accepted by both.

The hard work, preparation, homework, and extra mile work had paid off. I went on to attain my bachelor's degree at Rowan and was thankful for the hard lessons that failure had taught me, and it wouldn't be the last time. Unfortunately, my dad didn't get to see it but where my career and technology have taken me, I was able to say that I attended Wharton. I was able to because now there are things like online classes, and I have a company that cares enough about me to invest in my success. It wasn't the way we thought, but we made it dad.

Integrity

Above all things, being a leader with integrity is a non-negotiable facet of having a leader's presence. When you are a leader, nothing is done in secret even if you think it is. It is certainly true that you can work on your reputation your entire life and destroy it within an instant. There is no such thing as a harmless indiscretion or a little white lie. Your people will see where you draw the line for yourself and use that very measure for themselves. It can't be, do as I say and not as I do.

Remember your career is like a stage and everything that you say and do is under a microscope for the world to see. It's much easier to hold yourself to the highest standards and you never need to worry about anything. It's easier than you think to hold the line when it comes to integrity, and it's easier than you think to fall away from that standard too. Don't take the bait, take the high road instead. As you continue to be a leader with integrity you continue to build your house of integrity one brick at a time.

 With this, understand that you and everyone else are human. So, if a mistake is made, then be quick to be truthful and admit your mistake and what you are doing to fix it. There are times when actions after the error can be worse than the error itself. So, in everything you do, do it with your integrity in mind. If you don't want to read about it in the news, chances are you shouldn't do it.

Of course, there can be many other facets to having a leader's presence. My intention here was to supply you with the ones that I feel are important and non-negotiable. However, the most important one would be the last one which is integrity. You might have all the other ones, however, if you don't have integrity, the other ones don't matter. These simple things that take no special talents will put you ahead of so many others in the pack. The others may be smarter or more educated or have more money, but these simple keys will mean more in the long run to your success. The only thing they take is desire and discipline on your parts to see them through and make them happen.

The Extra Mile

1. Make sure that your appearance matches your current position or even better the next level up.
2. Make sure that your speech meets the standard that you set for yourself and your position.
3. Always remain calm, remember that your team is looking for you to set the tone.
4. It's okay to lead with your heart, just be aware of the dangers.
5. Lead from the front when needed but don't micromanage.
6. Always be prepared.
7. Most importantly, ALWAYS lead with integrity.

LEADERSHIP

Volumes of works have been written on leadership throughout the ages. You can study leadership for a lifetime, yet you still cannot capture what it means to be a good leader. You can turn to books, websites, videos, coaches, you name it; there's someone who will be happy to tell you what their version of leadership is and charge you money for it. Obviously, in this book, my intention is not to teach you or postulate what leadership is or means. My purpose here is to write about what leadership means to me, how it has helped me in my career, how I have changed my thoughts on this topic, and how it has changed and grown as I have changed and grown.

Leadership is a double-edged sword as well. When it goes well, the results are evident for all to see. When it goes poorly, if you allow it, it can take a negative personal toll on yourself and those you lead. My business leadership journey began in 1995 when I was 22 years old and was thrust into a situation where I was unprepared for anywhere. In my first book, Success in Auto Body and Collision Shop Management, I spoke about the conditions that led to this. While I explained what happened and how it happened, I didn't talk about what helped me through that time. On paper, I should have failed quickly, and no one would have been surprised or would have blamed me for it. However, thanks to the support of others and some leadership training that I didn't even realize was leadership training, I could make it through. As I said at the close of my first book, "Above all, Lead!" No matter what the situation is, no matter what task, or even if you feel it's beneath you. I don't care if the mission is to remove the shop trash, then get out there and show everyone how it's done.

My first leadership lessons

The first person who provided me with leadership training in my life was my father. It's funny because he didn't have a classroom and didn't sit me down and say, it's time for me to train you on leadership. He just lived his life and set an example for me that I was able to absorb without even realizing it. My father was a strict, no-nonsense person and a hard worker. He was born to a working-class family where everyone was expected to pull their own weight. He told me two stories that I remember about how he grew up in South Philly. When my dad was younger, he would be told to go out with a bucket, pick up coal that had fallen off the train cars, and bring it home so the family could use this "free" coal for heat. The second story was also from his younger days; his family would go to farms and pick fruit and vegetables from the fields. My memory of him telling me this was that it was very embarrassing for him at the time, and people had made fun of them for having to do this "poor people's" work. I believe events like this made my father grow into the man and leader he became because of these poor beginnings. My father didn't go to high school; his father was a tailor, and his mother was a homemaker. They lived in a very Italian American neighborhood, half a block from the vegetable and fruit stands on Ninth Street in the Italian Market in Philadelphia.

A Decision

From these beginnings, and for reasons lost to time, my dad decided to go to a trade school and learn auto body repair at The Bok School, near his house. I can only imagine that he saw his future as that of a man working with his hands for the rest of his life. I'm sure he didn't stop to consider that the choice he was making would affect not only his life but the lives of his children and now grandchildren. I wish I knew more about this journey and how the story began. What I do know is that he learned the auto body trade and became very talented at it.

By the time I came on the scene in 1973, my dad had gone from body technician to auto body shop owner of a large two-story shop on Snyder Avenue in the heart of South Philly, which was the place that I grew up in and gave me the love and passion for this business. That shop grew to other shops in York, PA, Wrightstown NJ, Southwest Philadelphia, and Upper Darby PA. He also invested in other businesses, including furniture, beauty parlors, and men's shoe stores. It has always amazed me that he could accomplish these things from his humble beginnings. However, it did teach me that no matter where you come from, you can work hard and achieve great results. My father, like any man, wasn't perfect, and as a human, he made mistakes that cost him many of the accomplishments that he earned. All the while, through success and failure, as his son, I was watching. I learned that no matter what circumstances you come from or are in, you can change them through dedication and hard work.

The Lesson of the Glass Bookcases

I remember a lesson my father taught me one day as if it happened yesterday. My father had large glass bookcases in his office at the shop. I can still picture them today; they were probably 8 feet tall and 4 feet wide. The entire bookcases were glass, doors, shelves, and everything. Now, mind you, my dad was a heavy smoker; it seemed like everyone back then was. So, these bookcases used to get covered in the yellow coating from cigarette smoke. You probably know what I'm talking about if you grew up in the 70s and 80s. My dad approached me one day at the shop and said, "I want you to go to my office with the glass cleaner and clean my bookcases." In my mind, no factor, I'll get this done in 2 seconds. I grabbed the glass cleaner and paper towels and headed to his office. In less than 10 minutes, I was back in front of my dad, probably proud of myself at how fast I "completed" the mission and told him I was done. He asked if I checked my work and ensured there were no streaks, and everything was done correctly? "of course, I checked, and it's all good." "Ok, let's go to my office and see," my dad said. Now he knew what he would find, and I should have known better, but to his office we went.

We arrived at his office, and my dad examined every inch of the bookcases and yelled about how it wasn't acceptable. He went at me up one end and down the other, and the more he found, the angrier he got. There were streaks, missed spots, and plenty was wrong. My dad had a temper, and anything could set him off. He chewed me out for what felt like an eternity and told me to do it over again and do it right. I returned to work, being more careful and taking more time. I knew how mad he was, so I wanted to make sure I did it right, and I also wanted him to cool off. I took double the time this round and tried hard to ensure I did it right. Remember, these are substantial glass bookcases covered in a film of nicotine. Ok, I was ready this time and went back, hoping he would trust me. No such luck, and to his office again we went.

I think you know where this story is going. Of course, my efforts this time weren't acceptable either, or the next or the next. It felt like this up and down, going back and forth lasted forever. At that point, I thought my dad had enough and just let it go.

Each time I went back to work, I did better than the time before. I saw things I had missed and was more careful. Reflecting on this lesson today, as I have done many times, I realized something. If I could keep improving on the job I did each time, why did I feel I was finished the first time? Or the second, third, or fourth? If I had done it right in any of those times, I wouldn't have been able to improve upon them. The truth is, I hadn't done it right at those times; I was rushing to get it done, and I was accepting less-than-stellar work. My dad didn't take that. This day's lesson of a few hours is probably in my mind from 40 years ago and still teaches me. It has taught my children, and I hope it teaches you something too. Do any job right the first time, no matter how insignificant it may seem. Work to do your best in everything and ensure it's done right. You don't get extra credit for speed if you must do it over or it wasn't done correctly.

As a father or leader, your life and actions are on stage for all to see. Your children see and understand more than you realize, as do the people you lead. Again, your words are meaningless if they aren't in step with your actions. As a leader, if you are having a bad day, everyone knows it, even if you try to hide it. If you aren't committed or believe in something, you tell them, and they know it no matter what you say. Leadership of others is the highest honor for a leader and the most prominent mountain that some of us will face. When leading people, it's almost not okay to be a human anymore. Sometimes, you can't show human emotions anymore because you are held to a higher standard. You also can't have an ego or take things to heart. As a leader, you need to be above all those things now. People are allowed to take advantage of you and treat you poorly. Good leaders, though, don't take things personally and don't hold onto past grudges. It's better and easier just to let them go. The leader handbook doesn't explain these things because there isn't one.

My dad was a strong-willed man's man, if there ever was one. He set the standard for me regarding how to carry myself as a man and a leader. For a long time, I felt I could never hold myself up to the standard he set for me. I am so grateful I had such a fine teacher and an example of who and what to aspire to. I believe most of the problems of this world today can be traced back to the lack of leadership and positive examples in the world today. How can you know how to conduct yourself if no one taught you and you have no examples to follow? I was blessed to have a great example, and my duty was to teach and share that with my children, which I have done and continue to do. Not only my dad but I also have been an avid reader my entire life, and I have had a passion for military history.

From as early an age as I can remember, I filled my time with reading about American military history. My favorite areas of study were the American Civil War and World War Two. Imagine all the examples of leadership found within those two conflicts. I have studied leaders such as Dwight Eisenhower, Robert E. Lee, George Patton, and Stonewall Jackson. I studied and learned their good and bad points, and each has influenced my life. Imagine how high the stakes that their leadership depended on were. I have never faced stakes as high as they would. My father's example and their example forged the leader and the man that I am today. By no means am I perfect; no one is. However, through my study and their example, I became a person who is tough and stoic. So, when thrown into trying situations, I tried to remember that a tough day at the shop would never come close to being as stressful or as challenging as what the men that I studied throughout history had endured. Their example had gotten me through the tough days at the beginning of my career when I didn't know what I was doing as I wrote about in my first book.

> *To be an effective leader, you must be an effective communicator*

Effective communication is one of the keys to effective leadership. People cannot know what is happening in your head and what you think. All too often, leaders assume that we know what they are thinking. To be an effective leader is to be an effective communicator. I've learned that you shouldn't make assumptions no matter how clear you feel about the situation, and you may have to explain things differently. What I mean by that is that one size does not fit all in communication. You may explain something in what you think is crystal clear fashion, but the message didn't get across as you anticipated. People often use the wrong answer, raising their voices or becoming argumentative or angry. Once that happens, the actual message is lost and forgotten, and now we focus on the fact that you and I are in a confrontation.

Again, I'll give you another example of what I mean: a true story about my dad. He was a hell of an intelligent guy and had a mathematical mind. In seconds, he could look at a financial statement and know what he saw and what it meant. It was uncanny how good he was with math. As I told you, I am a history lover; I wasn't a math lover. Math doesn't come naturally to me. I remember many times in grade school when I hoped not to get called to the front of the class to work out a problem on the blackboard. (Showing my age with that one) The math didn't come naturally to me, and I had to think things through. Much of it didn't make sense other than basic math.

When I needed help with my math homework, I would go to my dad because I knew he was so good at it. However, that's where we ran into a communication problem. My dad would take one look at my homework and, in seconds, would see the answer. On the other hand, I would look at the page and see a foreign language. The longer it would take me to figure things out, the angrier he would be. The angrier he would get, the more nervous and longer it would take me to get the answers.

What we had was a communication issue. My dad wasn't communicating what he saw on the page for me to understand because he understood instantly and assumed I did, too. I wasn't communicating what and why I wasn't understanding, resulting in anger and frustration. After a few times, I avoided going to him for help, and my math grades continued to suffer.

Here is another true story from earlier in my career. I was

in the shop and approached a car with the hood open. I was looking in the engine bay, and suddenly, the horn went off, and it scared the you know what out of me. Two technicians were working in and around the car, and I thought they had done it on purpose. So, being the young hothead that I was, I got into a heated confrontation with them. The next thing I knew, they were closing their toolboxes and walking out as I continued to yell.

 Shortly after that, the boss called me to ask why I had made his two best techs quit. The techs returned, but only after I was gone, and never to return. I'm one of those who seems to learn the hard way with everything. This was no different, and I learned the hard way on this one, too. They didn't know I was standing there, and I didn't think they were inside the car diagnosing a horn that wasn't working. All of this could have been avoided, and my costly lesson could have been skipped if I had communicated effectively and hadn't lost my temper. Not everyone will understand what you are trying to get across. Try another communication method if your message isn't unclear on the first try. Lastly, don't get angry when someone doesn't understand. You just might not be speaking their language.

Another part of being an effective communicator is knowing when it's essential to communicate with the group and when it's time to talk one-on-one. Everyone should know by now that you should praise in public and correct in private. That's a no-brainer, and you need to make sure that you remember this even when you may be angry or frustrated. But when you have something important to share, you should communicate more deeply. I have often stood in front of a group or gotten on a call where I felt I was being crystal clear, and there was no way that anyone didn't get the message. I was clear and concise; I understood it, and so should everyone else.

Who couldn't have understood something so clearly laid out? The answer is plenty of people. This is like when I was in the math classroom, and the teacher asked, "Does anyone not understand?"

I didn't raise my hand because I didn't want to look stupid in front of my classmates, so I kept it down. Repeated and clear instructions are the best way to convey your message. Not only that but giving it out on multiple platforms is also essential.

 For example, if I wanted to share a new message with the team, I would most likely give it out in the following manner. I would put it out on my monthly kickoff Teams meeting with the entire team. I would also book time to discuss it at my Regional Manager's weekly Team meetings. I would book time at each Regional Manager's live monthly meetings. I would visit the centers and discuss things in small group settings. I would then follow up with personal and team meetings for any center or teammate struggling with the results.

Always explain the "why."

Explaining why is of the utmost importance in getting your message across. I used to think earlier in my career that if I understood it, so should you. But over time, I recognized the flaw in this thinking, just like I wish my dad had when going over my math homework. Don't forget that we are all unique individuals. We each have a unique history and knowledge that no one else can share. What might be obvious to you might be foreign to me.

 The key is to explain the why behind what you are telling me. If you give me the why and the story behind it, it will help me to understand why you want me to do something and understand it better. I may consistently say that we must ensure that we take vehicles apart one hundred percent for the estimate to be written. To me, that is self-explanatory and almost insulting to need to explain further. However, I am giving the message from the perspective of having grown up in the business and having managed it for almost thirty years. I may be speaking to someone with two years of experience, and it isn't so obvious. But it will be much easier to understand if I take the time to explain why it's essential and the benefits when you do, and the detractors when you don't.

Ex-Navy Seal Jocko Willink and his leadership consulting company, Echelon Front, speak at length about explaining the why. Always take the time to explain the "why." It will be worth your time.

Where are you setting the bar?

Having high standards is also essential. I have found that whatever level you set the bar to, that is where people will strive to go, but not further in most cases. I don't know why things are this way, but maybe it's like when you have a deadline to meet for a project. If the deadline is two months away, most people won't do anything until it is looming, and then they get moving after doing nothing for most of the time. I have never been that way. If given a task, I want to get it done and off my plate. I never believed in having an "in box" with things piling up. I want the inbox to be empty and ready if something unexpected arrives.

Here is another easy example. I was running a shop, and it seemed like the monthly sales plan would be very difficult to hit. However, my boss put out a bounty that whoever could not only hit the plan but exceed it by ten percent would get a $200 gift card. Suddenly, not only was the budget attainable, but there was no way I wasn't getting the gift card either. What changed? My mindset changed, and I said I beat the budget by more than ten percent.

Have you ever heard of the Law of Limited Performance? Paraphrasing, this law states that once a person understands the level of performance that will be expected from them, they stop trying to do better. Then, once their leadership sees this, they think that is all the person is capable of, and they stop trying to get more out of them. All the while, each person is responsible for continuing the cycle of not getting better. I could never be accused of not setting the bar high enough. Time and time again, it has been proven to me that if you put the bar high, people will work toward that goal and accomplish the mission. Here is how I have always thought about this. If I am going to leave home and work every day, why not be the best I possibly could be? Either way, I will be away from my family and work. Why make that sacrifice to come in nineteenth place? It never made sense why some people didn't care what the scoreboard said. In anything I do, I want to be or my team to be the best. In almost every case, the expenditure of effort is either the same or slightly more; that's it. Think of a NASCAR race; the difference between the winner's circle and tenth place is fractions of a second, and that's after driving five hundred miles.

Different skills at different levels of leadership

Many leaders that I know today made their way up through the ranks. They did good work in the office, so they became general managers. They did good work as general managers, so they became regional managers. What can become a problem is a high performer's tendency to work and get things done themselves. My ability to outwork the next person made me successful in my career. I was willing to put in whatever time it took to complete the job. This worked well before I was a general manager, and even to a degree as a general manager. I could still step in personally when needed to handle a task.

However, the problem is that when working for hands-on something, you can lose track of many other things that require your attention. For instance, the detail department backs up, so you do what you feel is right and start washing cars. That's admirable; sometimes, that may be the right thing. But you must be cautious. I say this because if you turn your back on everything to wash cars, then other things that you won't be there to correct may go wrong.

I am recalling a scene from the HBO miniseries Band of Brothers. In the scene, Captain Richard Winters, played by Damien Lewis, oversees the whole battalion and watches a failed attack from Easy Company and their then-commander, Lieutenant Dike. His first and natural reaction is to unsling his rifle and begin running to the action to take over. However, he quickly remembers that he oversees the whole battalion and can't leave those responsibilities to take over one attack. He quickly recovers, looks around, sees another officer standing right there, and commands him instead to take over the failed attack. So, if you need to handle something personally, just be aware of what is happening around you so that when you come back to your overall view, you check on what you may have missed.

This can happen on a larger scale when you are a regional manager. The further you move away from the front lines, the harder it is to make an impact yourself. To continue growing, you need to develop new skills, not the ones you found successful in your current role. As you progress from general manager to regional manager, you must resist the order of being a superman or woman and take everything on your shoulders. Imagine a shop with ten to fifteen employees. Now imagine each of those employees coming to you with their problems. You may be tempted to say, "Don't worry, I can handle that." Now, if you did that for everyone, by the end of the day, you would have a pile of ten to fifteen tasks that need to be completed while you watch all those people go home for the night; you are stuck there.

On a regional manager level, now you have that same number of employees, but now times six to eight businesses. It's impossible to keep doing things yourself, but people still try and fail. I don't remember where I heard this quote, but I will paraphrase it because it rings true. The coach doesn't go into the game when the quarterback is injured and start throwing the ball. That's not what the coach is there for. Again, how many things can go wrong in other places if the coach is tied up in the game throwing the ball?

Another thing that I learned from Jocko Willink and his best-selling books is that there are only two kinds of leaders: effective and ineffective. That indeed cuts through a lot of the red tape and metrics. So, when you look in the mirror at night and want to know what kind of leader you are, ask yourself and your team- Am I effective or ineffective?

Follow me

The next topic that I am going to talk about seems like it should be common sense but believe me from what I have seen it is not. In order for people to follow you, you actually need to be available and lead them. I'm not sure why, but I have run into more than one leader who just hides in plain sight not making themselves available and waiting for there to be a problem and maybe they step in. Leadership is active and dynamic. It's an all-day everyday responsibility that doesn't take time off. Leaders lead, that's what we are here for. As Major Dick Winters from the famous true story of the Band of Brothers said: "If you're a leader you lead the way. Not just on the easy ones, you take the tough ones too."

There is never a moment in leadership where you "make it." No matter how much you accomplish or think you are growing closer to a goal or moment, it never actually comes. This is true in all areas of leadership, from the store level to the regional level, and onward to the state or multi-state areas. I used to use the example that leadership is like chopping down a tree. You've worked hard and the chips have been flying all day. You come to the end of a day or a week thinking that when I come in tomorrow, I have just a little work left and the tree will fall in the morning. Then you arrive in the morning only to find that the tree is whole again. Similarly, regional or state leadership is like trying to chop down an entire forest.

 The lesson is that the tree never does fall, and the forest never does get cut down. Each day, you need to bring your best and work hard. There never is an end to leadership and you will never see the mission to completion.

I also want to point out that your career as a leader knows no ending. There is no position or title to attain that will enable you to finally sit back and put your feet up and relax. Each position or title only means a new challenge and new responsibilities. At a store level, you may be responsible for twelve to fifteen people. In a regional one, one hundred to one hundred twenty or more. At a state or multi-state level then two hundred fifty to five hundred or more. This is a great responsibility and should be treated as such. At each of these levels, you must grow your skills and grow yourself. Unfortunately, it's easy to spot leaders who have grown one level or more past where they should have stopped.

I have seen leaders like this react in two ways. The first is anger and frustration where they come to yelling and belittling their people instead of leading them. They like to point the finger and wish they could just have better people on their team. Real leaders point the finger at themselves and put the onus for success squarely in their lap. The second reaction that I have seen is hiding in plain sight. Since some leaders don't know what to do, they just abandon their posts and can't easily be found. They are somewhere but they can't easily be seen or heard. They aren't at the front, they aren't leading. If you look for them you may be able to find them, but they just exist, they don't lead.

Leading means being seen and heard. Leading means putting yourself, and your thoughts and ideas out there. Leaders aren't afraid to share their ideas and plans to make things better. However, when you aren't afraid to do those things, you must be ready for people to throw stones at you. Think about Theodore Roosevelt's famous The Man in the Arena speech. It's easy to be those un-named people on the sidelines but it takes character to be standing in the area. You owe it to those who you lead to climb into the area and be seen and heard. If you don't dare to do that then you don't deserve to have the honor of being a leader and should step down.

I'll never understand how someone in a position of leadership stands idle while watching someone on their team headed the wrong way. Yes, I understand that people need to learn and do things for themselves. But at the same time would you watch someone you care about walk into a dangerous situation and not warn them? Wouldn't you at least caution them and make sure they have thought about the potential areas that might cause them harm?

There is a difference in leading someone and doing it for them and going too far either way has its dangers. It is dangerous to be a micro-manager and do things for people and it is dangerous doing nothing and leaving people on their island. Whether I succeed or I fail, I would rather do it knowing that I did everything that I could for the people I am honored to lead. I want them to know that I care about them as people and about the career and their personal success. To do that, I need to be invested and involved in them. To invest in someone and see them succeed and grow is the greatest repayment for any leader.

Going the extra mile

1. Remember your first leadership lessons.
2. The lesson of the glass bookcases.
3. Good leaders know how to communicate.
4. Always take the time to explain the why of what you are asking for.
5. Wherever you set the bar, that's where people will strive for.
6. Different levels require different leadership skills.
7. Be a leader that others will follow.

LEADERSHIP PITFALLS

Unfortunately, or fortunately, depending on how you look at it, I have had more bad examples of leaders in my career than good ones. However, this also taught me many lessons that I incorporated into my leadership style. Something must be taken away and turned into good in almost any situation. The advantage of having bad bosses is that they can teach you what not to be in many cases, and that's how they taught me. There were also times when I wasn't the leader I should have been either.

Pitfalls to watch out for

One thing I don't like is "seagull" bosses. You know, the ones who come in and scream and yell, leave their droppings on you, and fly off. One boss stood out when I was a General Manager. I ran a highly successful shop, and the store metrics were among the best in the business's entire portfolio of shops, which was sixty-six stores at the time. Our team was crushing it in every metric, and we had a tight-knit group that got along very well. Everything was how it should have been, and I was even asked to speak at several meetings about what we were doing that was making us so successful. So, when my boss came by, he would be frustrated about not being able to find anything to complain about. Which, of course, should have made him happy.

Unfortunately, it didn't make him happy and may have threatened his ego. So, his tactic was to walk around until he could find some supposed minor infraction on which he could get the store and myself. On one occasion, after everything looked good as it usually did, he went into my technician's bathroom in the shop, and his infraction was that it was dirty. While technically, he was right, and by the letter of the law, I deserved to have that documented. But with everything else going right and being outstanding, he only did this to find something to complain about. This did not endear my team or me to him or his leadership tactics. Unfortunately, it seemed that his ego would not allow someone to perform at a high level or was possibly a threat to him.

The next one I will discuss is tough because this person is a highly successful multi-shop owner. It is tough because he broke so many leadership rules, but he is highly successful money-wise as I mentioned. The lesson is that you shouldn't believe your positive press sometimes because it can change who you are as a person. I can honestly say that while I am not perfect, I do care about people and would never want to turn into someone who doesn't. This boss taught me so many things about not being a leader; again, I am thankful for the lessons he taught me, but he taught me what not to do. And who I did not want to be. He did open my eyes though as how fast a shop could run and how far you could push people whether that was good or bad.

Respect other people's time

First, there are just some basic things he did that you should never do. For starters, he always showed up late for anything and everything. By doing that, he clarified that your time wasn't valuable, but his time was. He furthered that trend by calling and texting after normal business hours and expecting you to be at his beck and call. He also scheduled live meetings for after the close of business or on weekends. These are basic things that any good leader should abide by. If you are on time, you are late; if you are early, you are on time. Never be late, as everything is in your control. Even traffic isn't an excuse; you should have planned for that and could have prevented it. Making people wait for you is a blatant disregard for their time, which goes for meetings, calls, whatever. It is also important to remember that people's time away from work is their time, and you, as a good leader, should respect that. This should only be violated with an apology if there is a true emergency they can only help with. Violating someone's private time again shows you don't value their time or them and that you are more important.

Praise in Public and correct in private

Everyone knows that you should praise in public and correct in private. However, he didn't believe that either. He made a show of correcting someone and would ensure he had as big an audience as possible. He would show up unannounced to a location and gather the entire office staff, where he would walk to each vehicle and ask questions rapid-fire. Depending on his mood or the point he was trying to make, he would keep going to make the person under scrutiny look stupid in front of their whole team, and then he would disappear as fast as he arrived for everyone to pick up the pieces. If he had performed this exercise differently, it might have had value. But it wasn't a constructive exercise because his goal was to belittle, embarrass, and make himself look like the know-it-all. He wanted me and others to do it to others as well, just like he did. I hated having it done to me, so I never wanted or enjoyed doing it to others and never made it personal or embarrassing.

What was accomplished was to embarrass and belittle the person who was the target and show everyone that there was only one true boss: him. What kind of respect did that person's team have for them after they saw their leader belittled? None. Now, they all saw if they wanted anything, they had to come to him instead of their direct leader, which broke the chain of command. The chain of command is important and should be respected unless someone tries to do anything unethical, illegal, or immoral. There are plenty of times when I am contacted directly by someone. My first question is, have you always brought this to your general manager or regional manager? I will then ask them if we can include them in the conversation. Unless they can explain why, I always bring them in and include them.

If I don't, I am effectively chopping them down and showing everyone that they don't need to go to their direct leader and they can come to me.

I have no desire to cut my leaders out as I don't care about my ego, and I don't need to cut them down to lift myself. By disrespecting your other leaders, you show everyone else that it's okay to do that, too. It's cheap, so don't do it. Belittling people for no reason, or any reason helps nothing. You don't help, guide, or motivate people by belittling them. Fear is a poor and short team motivator. If you get results, it's only if you continue to do it, and it's only until that person can get away from you. A relationship based on power needs power to continue, and it won't last. There were also times when he would announce that he would take over running your operation for some time.

However, he would come with a caravan of extra people. He would divert other employees from his other shops to bring with him. So, it wasn't an apples-to-apples comparison with the additional resources he brought with him. So, when he decided to leave and take all the extra people with him, he acted like he showed everyone how it was done. However, he only showed what could be accomplished by bringing all these extra people from other places would be accomplished and that vanished as soon as he left. The point that he tried to make as usual was how great he was and why didn't you do the things he did.

Earlier, I mentioned that he liked to call meetings whenever he wanted. He would make everyone stop what they were doing, no matter how busy they were. He would direct everyone to the conference room and wait for him. Depending on how long he felt like it, you would sit there waiting, knowing that you would need to stay late to finish your tasks. When he did show up, most of his conversations were about how great he was and how he accomplished so much. In these meetings, too, he would single people out in front of everyone for what, in his mind, they did wrong. You may have difficulty believing it, but these things happened. I would sit there in disbelief as these meetings could go on for hours, and well after, you should have left for the day.

His ego wouldn't allow anyone else to be the story's hero. It had to be him; there was no other room for anyone else. If he felt that anyone had the team's respect or was becoming too successful, he would make it a point to belittle them or transfer them to other locations. Here's the thing: He paid well, and because of that, he felt that you would deal with all these things. A true leader wants to build more leaders, not more followers. In addition to that, when leaders you mentored succeed and are promoted, it is a tribute to you and not a detractor. I had the respect of many of the people in this organization. This as the owner should have made him happy but unfortunately that wasn't the case. It made it worse for me because his professional and personal jealousy wouldn't allow it. I felt more and more of an outcast. Wherever I was, he would never go to that shop. He would make sure to ghost the shop that I was working in and go to all the others, taking people out on work time and socializing.

Don't play Favorites

One of his worst things was playing favorites and using his influence to play people against one another. He put me in charge of the company but then used two others who were in his inner social circle to make sure I didn't have too much power, I guess. Even though I was supposed to be in charge he would keep in tight with these two other guys and socialize with them as well. He made it clear by doing this that the chain of command didn't matter and that he was the real person of power in the company.

How can you lead a company when the owner uses people as pawns and makes sure everyone knows that their loyalty must be his? I was loyal to him, so he didn't have anything to worry about.

By playing people against each other and showing and removing his favor he kept everyone chasing after him and it was an effective but sad use of what could have been a great company to work for. While he has been successful, he could have been even more so because his employee turnover is huge and so many great and talented people have been through his door, but he doesn't hold onto the talent that he should. In his mind, I'm sure he sees nothing but success. However, is success on the backs of others for his gain.

Adversity

While the focus of this chapter so far has been on the flaws of other leaders and what I learned not to be. I would be a fake and a liar if I also didn't focus on my leadership shortfalls and the lessons that they taught me the hard way. When I was working for the organization, I just mentioned, it changed who I was as a leader and the person that I wanted to be. With the constant pressure, having every day feel like it was an emergency, and the constant threat of losing my job, it changed who I was. When I talk about it today, I compare who I was at that point to Darth Vader. Oh yeah, I got results and lots of them, but I didn't care who I had to run over or who I had to hurt that got in my way. I became a cold, callous machine only caring about looking for results. That's what that organization wanted and praised.

There came a point where I was working seven days a week because I was afraid that the owner was going to find something, anything to complain about. The culture of fear was everywhere, and I didn't want to lose my position or my job. This place was infamous for firing people, cutting their pay, or transferring them to other locations no matter where they were. I remember telling my wife that I had to go in on Sunday to get the this or that ready because I didn't want the owner coming and finding some alleged fault on Monday. I was fighting for survival and all the while turning into someone that I didn't want to be.

That's the weird part. I didn't like the culture or the way that I was being treated but I turned into someone I didn't want to be too. The pressure and the culture were not an excuse, and I regret who I allowed myself to turn into. It was dog eat dog and somehow, I became a part of that way of doing things. Things needed to be done, and people were just a hindrance. If I needed something done, I got it done and people and their feelings didn't matter. It became either get this done or I will get someone else to do it. If I can't find someone to do it, I will do it myself and get it done better and faster.

The sad part is that it worked, and I was very good at it. I got results and the owner loved that about me. Here is a word of warning to watch out for. Just because you are getting results, don't be fooled. There are many bad short-term answers that you can reach to get results. That doesn't mean that you should though. Short-term answers and short-term results are rarely going to last for long. However, the price that you may need to pay from them may be. I didn't even realize what I had turned into, as I had become a product of my environment, and I hated the environment.

An after-effect of this was that I became this angry machine at home too. You can't just shut down after being Darth Vader all day. You come home and expect results too. So, I stormed in the front door and just like at work, if I didn't like what I saw, I lashed out. If I didn't like what was for dinner, I said something. If the house didn't look clean enough, I said something. If you name any other thing that I could have complained about, I did. I treated the people that I cared about the most, and that cared about me the most like they were hired hands there to do my bidding. And I didn't even realize it or mean it.

Only after I left this organization did I realize that I had slowly changed over the nine years that I had been there. After I left, my wife and kids slowly told me how different I was after I left that culture. I guess having the feeling of a piano hanging over my head for all those years and having every day treated like it was an emergency really had changed me. It was so nice not to be that guy anymore and become a person again. Looking back, I didn't even have any hobbies when I left there. All I did was work and think about work and sleep, that's it. Once I left, I became a person again and took on hobbies like cooking and reading which I had stopped because I didn't have any time.

I am sharing these things with you so that you might not make the same mistakes that I made or potentially risk losing in your life what I risked losing in mine. No job is worth the risk of losing those who you love in your life. Neither is any job worth changing who you are as a person and your loves and passions. To think of what I risked for that job and for the money it paid me makes me shudder. I am thankful to God that he saw me though and had patience and mercy on me when I was too blind to see what was right in front of my face.

A new beginning

However, I have mentioned that sometimes I learn things the hard way and sometimes it takes a lot to get my attention. The next chapter of my career shows how true that is. After I finally got out of the toxic organization, I was hired to be the collision director for a large local dealership in the area. They are well known in the area and are a large wholesale parts distributor. At the time they had three body shops. One near their main Chevy, and Mazda dealership close by. Another was a stand-alone shop which was much smaller, and finally a small dealership with a Bodyshop two hours away. Things went great from the start. There was a professional environment, and I worked very quickly and made improvements in the shops. Many dealers don't understand how to run body shops, and they fail. A body shop today cannot be run like the other dealership departments.

It was easy for me to help and guide these shops into being more profitable and productive and the results were impressive. All the raw materials were there and just needed someone to bring them together. Things went so well, and the owner was so impressed that he began taking me under his wing and sharing plans with me for the future. With the level of work, we increased out of the main dealer body shop he was able to close the older smaller shop that he had in the area and sell the property without losing any income. We also made changes to the other shop which was two hours away and that shop became more profitable as well.

Things were going great, and I was thrilled that I made the move from my old job. I was making more money, was happier, and was getting great results. Therein were the seeds of a new problem, I was feeling full of myself. All this success was making me feel invincible. The results and metrics just kept getting better and the team at the body shops and the owner was thrilled. Not everyone was thrilled though as I came to learn. There were a lot of long-term sacred cows at the dealership though and most of them came from the sales side. Some had been there over twenty years, and they didn't take kindly to this new hotshot getting all the attention. I didn't care though and kept being me and just chalked their feelings up to them just being jealous.

The owner then came to me with a plan. He was so happy with me; he could see me running the entire dealership. Again, this is a huge multi-OEM dealer that is well-established and does serious sales and profits. The owner was young and treated me like I was in his inner circle. This felt like a dream come true. I had escaped my previous job and had finally landed in a place where I was appreciated, and I was shining. Everything seemed perfect.

The owner said that he was going to send me to the NADA academy where dealers send leaders to learn about running dealerships. This was a six-week course in Virginia and was the gold standard for those in management positions in dealerships. He agreed to send me and to pay me for everything. He made it clear that he was investing in me and said that the goal was for me to take over when the current General Manager retired. To do that, I needed this education, and he would also make me the Fixed Operations Director. In that role, I would not only oversee the body shop but also three service departments and the detail department. This was an opportunity beyond my career dreams and all I could think of was running a dealership, and the money that would come with it.

True to his word the owner sent me to the academy and made me the Fixed Operations Director. The change from just auto body to service wasn't an easy one but I was committed to learning and making it work. Now I had an office in the main dealership and was exposed to those long-term employees daily.

I also learned that even though the fixed operations of a dealership pay the bills. The variable or sales side is what garners the headlines and that's what dealers do; they sell cars. This position put me on equal footing with the General Sales Manager who had been there twenty-seven years and was the heir apparent to the General Managers seat until I showed up.

He and I clashed from the beginning. He was loud and condescending and I didn't like the lack of professionalism that he carried himself with. From the beginning, he had clashed with me even at the body shop, where he wanted things done cheaper and ahead of the paying customers who were our bread and butter. I always stood up for my department and never bowed down to him and I made it clear that I didn't like the way he conducted himself. Now we were in even closer proximity to each other, and we were both vying for the next position.

Humility was not a strong suit for me at this time. Everything I touched since I had been there had turned to gold and the owner had set a path for me who was this other guy to get in my way, no one informed him who I was around here.

During this time, I hired a good friend of mine to run the body shop from my previous employer. This guy was a great manager, and I knew he would do great things there while I focused on the service departments and getting the next promotion. I had tried for a long time to get him to leave where he was and to convince his family that making the move with me was the right move. Finally, he decided to come, and this was just another in a series of wins for me. I also graduated from the NADA Academy and things were going well in the service departments too. It seemed like I had the Midas touch with everything I did since arriving there. A couple of things happened, and I should have seen the signs or maybe I did, and I didn't want them to be true.

The owner who had lived in the area had bought another large group of dealerships in the Boston area and moved up there to work on them. I went from seeing him and talking to him several times a week to never seeing him and hardly talking to him anymore. The current GM who I was going to allegedly replace was solidly in the camp of the General Sales Manager and I think he also considered me an interloper. With the owner not around, I felt like I lost my protector and felt more and more dislike from the others in the dealership. I didn't care at the time and just felt they were jealous. I did not attempt to get to know them or understand their perspective. Point blank, I didn't care, I thought I was invincible.

Shortly after the owner called me and asked if I had any interest in moving up to the Boston area and working up there. Feeling full of myself, I said it depended on what he wanted to offer me as that was a big move on my part and he would have to offer the "golden handcuffs" if I was going to consider it. Also, he had shared his personal iTunes movie library with me which had over a thousand movies. Suddenly I no longer had access to it, I thought it must have been a technical glitch.

I started pushing the General Manager that I wanted to learn more about the sales side as I was ready for the next level. All the while my relationship with the General Sales Manager was more and more contentious. We oversaw separate halves of the dealership, yet we couldn't stand each other and didn't work together on anything. The only time I heard from him was when he wanted to complain about something. All the while I figured I was good, and I was protected by the owner and doing what he wanted me to do.

Be humble

Then came D-Day where it all unraveled. It was a Saturday, and I wasn't working, I was home when I received a message on our work messaging app. It was the General Sales Manager complaining again about the speed at which we were turning around his used cars for sale. Now mind you we had slashed the time it took to get him his cars back in half, but he never acknowledged or thanked us. Now here we were on my day off complaining again and using unprofessional, rude, and disrespectful language to me.

I should have just let it go, I was off and could have addressed it on Monday. Or if I was going to answer now, I could have composed myself and calmed down before giving him a measured and professional response. I did neither of those things, however. I was furious, I was seeing red, and I was going to put this guy in his place once and for all. I seethed with righteous indignation as I began to furiously type my response. I didn't use foul language,

I just told him I wasn't going to respond to him until he learned how to act and speak like a professional.

I guess he didn't appreciate the wit of my response. After I hit the send button, I immediately regretted it, but once the button was clicked it was sent, there was no going back.

At first, it seemed like everything was ok and nobody said anything when I went back to work on Monday. Tuesday was good too and I felt like maybe this guy finally got the message to not mess with the likes of a guy like me. The first hint of trouble came on Wednesday. Wednesday was the day that I went to the General Manager and had my weekly meeting with him. I would go to his office and brief him on everything I had going on. Since mostly everything I usually had going on was good, this should be a cakewalk.

As I pulled out my notes and began going over things he stopped me and said I wouldn't need my notes. That was odd but I'm sure I smiled and said okay no problem, expecting that he had something that he wanted to go over. He proceeded to tell me that I was no longer the Fixed Operations Director and that I would be going back to the body shop. I didn't quite understand because none of this made any sense. For starters, we only had one body shop at that moment as the owner had sold the dealership two hours away and we didn't need the small shop anymore since the big shop was doing so well.

As I sat there shocked and not understanding, I think I mumbled something to the General Manager like does the owner know about this? How could he? We had a plan, and I was just following the plan he gave me. I didn't understand what happened or what it all meant or what I was going to do.

I went back to my nice dealership office stunned and started boxing up my things. So, one minute I went from being King Midas and about to be promoted to a dream job and collecting my things in a cardboard box, going back to the body shop.

I probably got back to the old dingy body shop desk that I had started at and sat there staring off into space. I knew I needed to get in touch with the owner as surely, he would straighten this out. The problem was that he had become more and more out of touch with me and the once strong relationship that we had now seemed distant and strained. I called and emailed him and couldn't contact him. The General Manager's words didn't make sense to me. There was nothing for me to do in the body shop. I had made the improvements, and it was doing great. In addition, the manager I put in, my friend, was exactly what the place needed, and he didn't need any oversight from me. Thursday went by like a blur and I still tried to contact the owner thinking this all was somehow a mistake.

On Thursday the owner contacted me and said he would talk to me that night. After work, I waited, and the call finally came around 7 pm. Right off the bat, the once friendly and praising owner was quiet and distant. He gave me no explanation and didn't mention the General Sales Manager. Just that this was the decision and that's it, my position had been eliminated. As I heard him talking it seemed like I was in a dream world, and I couldn't believe how fast things changed. I told him that there was nothing for me to do in the body shop and that we had a manager, and it didn't require two. That's when he hit me with the ultimatum. "There's one body shop job, if you want it you will have to fire the manager." At that point, I knew it was over. I told him that the manager was my friend, and I convinced him to come and that I wouldn't fire him. I remember after hanging up, walking out of my office like a zombie and telling my wife it was over and that I was going to bed.

How did things change so quickly? How did I go from the top of the mountain to the bottom that fast? How did a dealer see how much I did to make their operations better, get promoted, get promises, and then be treated this way? The next day, I did something that I had never done in my career, I called out sick. Truth is I wasn't physically sick, but I sure was mentally sick, and I didn't know what was going to happen or what I would do. If ever I needed a mental health day this, was it. I couldn't believe how things changed so quickly. I felt lied to and used for my efforts and my knowledge and now the owner who had hired me turned on me.

I didn't know what was going to happen, but I showed up bright and early to work on Monday as I always did, too early perhaps. It was probably no later than 6:30 am as I set my things on my desk and turned my computer on. No one else was in yet, which was to be expected at that time. I heard the door open and wondered who could be coming in so early. When I saw the dealership General Manager walk in who never came to the body shop I knew it was over. He really didn't need to explain but he proceeded to tell me I was fired and to gather my things and leave while he watched. Wow, after everything I had done for that place, showing them how to make money and lots of it in the body shop and improving their service departments too. As I drove off into the unknown, I was lost, afraid, angry, sad, scared and many other emotions too. I pointed the finger at the owner, the General Manager, the General Sales Manager, it was all their fault. Or was it?

Extra Mile Work

1. Respect other people's time.
2. Praise in public and correct in private
3. Don't play favorites

4. Short term tactics get you short term results
5. Family first
6. Beware of your success
7. Be humble

The Wilderness

The time after I had been fired was the lowest point in my professional career. You see my job wasn't just what I did, it was also who I was. So, without my job, I had also effectively lost my identity. I was so focused on gaining the title of dealership General Manager, that had consumed me. In my adult life as a husband and a father, there had never been a time when I didn't have a high-paying and successful job. Now I was jobless and had no identity. This was not a familiar feeling to me, and I sunk into a state of fear and depression. I was a Regional Manager or a Director level for so many years, that's what I was used to. Well, not too many of those jobs exist in the collision industry so I wasn't prepared and hadn't had to look for a job unexpectedly for almost twenty years. Well, I needed to figure it out quickly as I had a mortgage to pay and a family to provide for just like anyone else.

I was used to being at work before 7 am and busy accomplishing things all day. Now I had nowhere to go and nothing to do. I was lost, there is no better way to put it. I began working on my resume and putting the word out that I was looking for a job. I knew that I was a collision industry leader at heart, and I had no desire to return to a dealership or service department. That's not who I was. I wanted to get back to where I felt comfortable and not like an imposter as I did in dealership fixed operations.

There was a local multi shop owner that I spoke to first and I was thankful for the opportunity. However, I did not want to work for an owner-operator again and was still feeling that sting from my job that I had been in for nine years and the way that owner handled things. I was also speaking with the two largest national multi shop operators at the time as well.

A new start

In what felt like an eternity but was only a week and a half, I agreed to come to work for at that time was the nation's second-largest collision repair multi shop operator. The only thing was that I couldn't just come in at a regional or director level as, once again, I needed to prove myself. While I was thankful to have a job, I certainly wasn't happy to be starting on the store level again which I hadn't operated in for several years. It made me feel that I had gotten knocked down by several years and several levels. I was still mad and upset at my last job, but I pointed the finger squarely at others. The owner had abandoned me, the General Sales Manager had gotten me fired. I was angry, and I felt sorry for myself. All my years of hard work had landed me back where I started. Not only was I back at a store level, but I also didn't even have a store. I figured this was a temporary setback as surely, I would quickly show this new company what I could do and would be right back at a high level again.

I entered the new company and did everything a new hire needs to do. I wasn't sure where I would wind up and the new company wasn't sure either. While I thought it wasn't fair what had happened to me, I still wasn't appreciating what a gift I had been given. You see the person who hired me wasn't even supposed to have hired me. He was told that they weren't looking for anyone else at the time and that he should pass on hiring me. I am so thankful that he saw something in me and had the guts to go against what he was told to do by his superior.

Little did I know that, when after a few weeks I wasn't happy to find out that my first mission was to go and take over a shop in Philadelphia about an hour away. I guess I was still hoping that someone would realize who I was and the experience level that I had and just elevate me right off the bat.

I figured this would be a formality and I would show everyone what I was capable of and quickly be elevated back to what I thought was my rightful place of being a Regional or above manager. I didn't like the drive, or the shop, or the hours, or any of it for that matter. I was still looking at the world as if it had wronged me and it somehow owed me something. I had made it, and I was past this level, didn't anyone realize this? It's funny to think that was my attitude and I'm sure God found it funny too as I will share with you where he led me from there.

Nonetheless, I took over the shop and used all my experience to turn the shop in a positive direction. However, I still had in my mind that it would be a quick mission, and in no time the cavalry would be headed over the next hill to come and save me. After the first few weeks of shaking off the rust, the old familiar feeling of running a shop came back. The beautiful part was that by doing what I knew would work, I could see the shop starting to get where it needed to be too. As I wrote about in my first book, there are certain things to do when running a shop and you will usually be successful.

One day my oldest son came to work with me, and we took a photo together out in the shop. I didn't know it at the time, but that photo would come to teach me a valuable lesson. Looking back at that photo later I could see the pain, sadness, and fear that were still within me.

Remember, I had lost my identity. While it was true at this point, I had a job, I still didn't have my identity. I was still lost and hollow inside, and still pointing the finger at how unfair this all was. As the shop turned in the right direction, I looked for someone there to take over as I surely would be moving on to bigger and better things soon, or so I thought. I identified that person and began to pour into him and teach him the things that he needed to do to become the manager once I had made my departure. I had my attention set on what I saw as my way out. There was a position where I could be looking after three shops, one of which was the one I had just been working at. This seemed like a perfect steppingstone in the right direction for getting back where I wanted to be

Another setback?

At this point, I had been with the company for around five months, and I was itching again to get moving. I was happy when I found out that I would be allowed to look after those other stores too, so I went back to multi-unit management and figured it was about time that this new company saw the light of who I was.

During this time a new boss had taken over who worked below the guy who hired me. I met him for lunch and started my new position overlooking the three shops. I thought everything went well and we had a nice conversation and a good lunch. I was still feeling good when the new boss told me he wanted me to go to a different shop in Philadelphia. It was in a really bad area of town and even though it was physically closer to home it would take much longer to travel to because of traffic. On I went figuring that I would quickly help that manager get things going and I would be right back to where I wanted to be.

Then things started getting strange. My access on the computer to the other stores and some other rights were changed, which was weird. Then my title was changed back to General Manager and the person who had that role at that center that I was sent to was transferred somewhere else. How was I going to help the manager of the store if there was no store manager? I reached out to my supervisor and explained my frustration and confusion as to what was going on. In the meantime, I took over the shop and started again putting things in place to help the team. As I mentioned this store was in a bad area and it had a bad reputation in the company. It was known as a hard-luck shop in a place that few people wanted to work in. A manager from another store called and asked me who I had pissed off to be put there. I honestly had no idea and was still in denial thinking that it was all a mistake.

Nothing to look forward to?

My supervisor told the boss how I felt, and they both agreed to meet me at the shop to discuss. My thoughts were that I had done everything that he asked me to do and shown him my skills. Why would my punishment be to be sent to this terrible shop that no one wants to be in? As soon as the meeting started, I knew it wasn't going to end well for me. The boss's attitude seemed like he was pissed off that he even needed to come and explain this to me. He quickly and firmly ended any thought I had and told me I had no job other than to be the General Manager of this store, with no further explanation. Again, I was crushed. I wasn't going anywhere, and this was my new life. I was in a place and a position that I didn't want to be in and there was nothing to look forward to.

Again and again, I ran the past through my head and couldn't believe how fast or how far I had fallen. It seemed no matter what I did, I couldn't keep this boss happy. It could be sunny with blue skies and yet if I told him that he would disagree. In my mind, I had gone from having the Midas touch to quite the opposite and nothing was going my way. I wanted to quit, throw my keys at him, and walk out. But at that meeting, I told him how I felt, but was respectful and didn't allow my emotions to run away. I told him that the team there needed leadership and help, and I would stay for them and their success until they were taken care of.

That was the truth. The people there were good people and just needed a leader to show them how to do things and they would respond. I believe this was a slight turning point in our relationship and I believe that saying that and honestly believing that, brought me to good future things. Since I stayed respectful in our meeting, there was one thing however that I had to take care of before moving forward. I sat down and wrote a resignation letter to him, my supervisor, and the boss that had hired me.

It felt great to write and it felt even better when I hit the send button. I felt relieved when I sent it, there was just one thing though. Instead of sending it to the people I addressed it to, I sent it to my wife. First off it gave me the satisfaction of writing and addressing it to the people I would have sent it to.

But secondly, I had no plan and thought better of it. Thirdly and most importantly, I meant what I said that the people at the shop deserved leadership and someone to care about them. I still have that resignation and have gone back to it from time to time to read it again and remember that period of my life.

Focus on others

I was now officially the General Manager of that store with no other thoughts than to help that store and that team to succeed. I put my head down and I went to work and there was nothing else competing for my attention. There was no future or next job or thing to look forward to. The team rallied behind me, and I saw that all they needed and wanted was a leader who cared about them. I gave them the parameters to follow, and they got it done. Seeing your team rise to the occasion and put the work in to succeed is a gratifying thing to witness as a leader.

As a few months went by the store did a turnaround and was now solidly heading in the right direction. My supervisor came over to say I was doing a great job and that even the boss who had marooned me there had noticed. He admitted that he thought that I would quit when he had put me there but was happy to see what I was doing to help the store and the team. My supervisor also told me there was a need for a Regional Manager and my boss was considering me for it. I didn't let that affect me and I just kept working and kept my focus on the team there, that was all I cared about. The feeling of being completely focused on the success of others made a big difference for me and made me happy.

On my long drives to and from the job, started listening to audiobooks. A book that really got through to me was about servant leadership. Hearing this book really helped me to start reflecting on what had happened to me. It also helped me to take the focus off myself and instead focus on my team and their needs. I started to see things differently about what had happened to me and instead of me pointing the finger at others, I started to point the finger at myself. None of this happened overnight but as I had nothing but time while I was in traffic daily, it started to evolve in my mind, and I began to see things differently.

Lessons

I learned that the only thing that I can control in life is myself and my actions. I cannot control those of others no matter how much I may want to. So, getting mad at the owner that I had worked for or anyone else in the past is just a waste of time. Up until that point though that's what I had been focused on. That is how unfair those people had treated me and that I had been a victim. Looking at yourself as a victim is always a waste of time and accomplishes nothing. You can't learn anything this way as it's always someone else's fault. The things about hard lessons are just that, they are hard. Without the trouble and pain in this time of my life, I just wouldn't have gotten it and wouldn't have listened. I was just too damn hardheaded to listen. But God knew better as He always does and knew I would only respond if the lesson made it hurt.

Humility

My mindset shifted to what did I do wrong and how can I learn from that lesson. I reran the scenarios of what happened through my mind, this time with the advantage of hindsight. The biggest thing that I would have changed in my approach was humility. The dealership that I had worked at had been established for a long time and had many people who had been working there for over twenty years. I hadn't taken the time to build any relationships with anyone. I just went in and got to work and didn't care how anyone else felt. I figured the owner had my back and people were just jealous of that and my success. By ignoring them it gave them no opportunity to get to know me and for them to trust me and that all I cared about was the company's success as they did.

What I should have done was take the time to get to know them and what they cared about. It wouldn't have been hard as I saw them daily, but I was too focused on my own success for that. Dealerships have different departments that are focused on different things. However, there are times when these departments do need to work with each other. Had I been a better teammate and relationship builder, I could have built trust with them and worked with them better than I did. My aloofness and territoriality pushed people away and allowed them to make assumptions about me that may not have been true. I helped to build professional enemies at work that while they may have not been against me, they certainly weren't for me. So, if there were some against me, I didn't have the relationships there that might have stuck up for me.

It was harder when it came to realizing what I had done wrong with the General Sales Manager. From our first encounter I could see by the way he talked and presented himself that he would be hard to deal with. As I look back now, we probably didn't like each other for the same reasons, and our egos probably were whispering in our ears when we first met. We both were proud, used to doing things the way wanted and were successful. However, he had come through the ranks and had been there over twenty years, while I had just arrived. I'm sure he had been climbing the ladder there with the hope of becoming the General Manager there long before I ever arrived.

Relationship building

As the new guy I should have reached out to this veteran of the company. As the General Sales Manager he was second in command, and I should have lowered my ego and showed him the respect that his position called for. Had I done this and showed him deference, he probably would have lowered his ego too. Why did his abrasive tone bother me so much? Most likely my ego was bruised when he didn't bow down first to me for all that I had accomplished in the body shop. I should have let his demeanor speak for itself and I shouldn't have let it affect me. Was he right in the way he acted? No of course not. But guess what, he's there today as the General Manager and I am long gone. I had the power to humble myself and go to him and show him how much I wanted to help him and his department and then backed it up by action.

The indirect approach

Another term that Jocko Willink often speaks about is using the indirect approach. Just like head on attacks on a defensive position are usually very costly if they work at all. A better way is to look for an alternate route or a flank attack which works much more often and with less casualties. When I saw how strongly defended his position was, I should have backed off and looked for a better way. However, the old me was going to have none of that and I attacked headfirst and got my head cut off for it.

Even on that Saturday when he messaged me complaining wrongly about the speed it was taking us to service his cars, I had other better choices I could have made. First and easiest I could have ignored him. After all it was Saturday, and I wasn't working that day, and I could have put the phone down as if I had never seen it. Secondly, I could have agreed with him and told him I would find out what was happening on Monday and that I would come up with a solution. Or finally, I could have said I'll be right over. I could have taken a quick thirty-minute ride and heard him out personally and we could have together come up with a plan that would have been satisfactory to both of us.

Beware your ego

Why did I get so angry at him? The answer was because my ego felt bruised by his tone. My ego basically said he can't talk to you like that, who does he think he is? You can't let this attack go without a response. I fell for my ego hook line and sinker. Who knows, maybe if I didn't respond I would still be working there. Or maybe we would have tangled again and again. Here is what it comes down to. I needed to learn a lesson to be successful in the long run. The hard part was that I couldn't see it at the time, and it felt like my career was destroyed and would never come back. Since I had not learned anything by being fired, the lesson continued in my new job with my new boss. Since I was still not getting it and was only focused on getting back to where I thought I deserved to be, God took that away and I finally started paying attention.

Beware of success

I certainly didn't see it at the time but as I explained to you, I was used to success, and I was used to getting things done. From the job I was at for nine years, through the dealership experience, it was one success after another. While getting out of the toxic culture I had been in certainly helped me not to be Darth Vader anymore, I was still full of myself and my success. In the beginning, losing the job at the dealership was the fault of other people and not my own. However, as my downward career spiral continued, I began to question the fault of others and began to think about the fault of my own and hold myself accountable.

As I have mentioned before I believe in the tenants of Extreme Ownership as written about by ex-Navy Seals Jocko Willink and

Leif Babin. As I kept re-running the past through my head, I knew that what had happened to me wasn't the fault of others, it was my fault. I learned best from experience and this lesson hurt and it stuck, and it accomplished the mission. As I began to realize the same scenario was repeating in my career because I wasn't learning the lesson. At every job I had, there was always an antagonist, and I would always go head-to-head with that person. I didn't care and I wasn't afraid to fight fire with fire. I always chalked it up to jealous people and I wasn't going to change. My ego fueled my desire not to back down but to fight back.

As I began to see things in a different light, I was at peace by what happened, and this was my new life, and I had to build from here. Then the call came when I stopped striving for it and thinking about it. It was the boss, and he wanted to meet me that night for dinner. At dinner, he told me that he wanted to offer me the position of Regional Manager for eight stores. He warned me though that had I handled myself differently at the current store he would never be offering me this. I was over the moon happy and was so genuinely grateful that I began to look at my entire situation differently. It had been a long eight months of ups and downs, with plenty of time for self-reflection. Those eight months were a great learning experience and time that I needed to learn some very hard lessons as we just went over. While I hated enduring the lesson, what the lesson taught me was invaluable. Little did I know how much I needed it, but God knew, and he gave me a lesson in humility for my own good.

As I kept thinking, I realized that I did play a big part in my failures and the lessons that came from them. So, in this case, instead of being that way as I had in the past with my boss, I backed off and declined to fight. Instead, I retreated and focused on doing my job and the team. Had I gone head-to-head with him, either I would have sent that resignation to him, or he would have fired me. After that meeting I was beyond honored and humbled now to have the opportunity and gift to get back to regional management and share my knowledge and experience with others.

Just in time

Only a few months into my new adventure it was announced that my company was going to be merging with the largest multi shop organization in the country. At that time, it was also announced that all job changes and promotions were frozen until after the merger. My boss, who seemed to hate me in the beginning, had acted in the nick of time. Had he not promoted me when he did, there is no guarantee that I would be where I am today. Here's the other ironic thing: My boss wouldn't be in the picture much longer. The day that the merger was completed, he was let go and was no longer in the picture. As fast as he arrived in my life to help to teach me the lesson, he was gone. That convinced me even more that what seemed like a dark period in my life, was there for my benefit. God was working in mysterious ways, to help and get me ready for bigger things.

I joined the new company and continued to lead those eight stores for a total of three and a half years. During that time, and thanks to the great team I had around me, we were the highest producing group of shops in the entire Northeast. We were very successful together and it felt so rewarding to be a part of it. However, there were still lessons left for me to learn. You see, you never arrive as a leader. There is never a time where you have checked all the boxes, and you can finally relax having graduated and figured it all out. Eight stores grew to nine during covid and I noticed that when the pressure was on, I was visited by a person that I didn't want to see anymore.

Vader

I didn't notice it at first but sometimes pressure comes in waves. During those times of high pressure and high stress, my unfortunate natural reaction is anger. It's not that I meant it, I'm just partially built that way, I guess, it could be my Sicilian blood. Most times, I kept it under control but sometimes I didn't. My boss came to be and asked if I would take over another branch of the company in his region. This meant that I would be leading a mobile business in four states. This business was a new wing of the company and would partially need to be built from scratch and would partially be dismantling some of the ideas that were already in place.

As things got underway, I felt the pressure, the stress, and my anger increasing. I had learned enough though to know that I didn't want to go back to the old me. I didn't want to go back to being that angry Darth Vader leader. I didn't want to come home at night and be mean to the people that I loved and cared for most. The part that I needed to be careful of though was that guy got results. While I hated being him, he got things done. But I didn't want to go back to being that machine. It was time to look for help.

Finding Purpose

My supervisor and some other leaders had gotten to do a small leadership group event called an intensive. After that he began speaking about purpose and how he found his and it helped him. I really didn't understand what it meant at first. I thought my purpose was to make money or have good metrics, but I was wrong. Not understanding purpose or what mine was had a big impact on why having been fired was so devastating to me. You see, once I was stripped of my job and title, there was nothing else. Without them, I didn't even know what I was because I didn't know what my purpose was. At that time my fear was that because of this added pressure, I would regress into the old me and ruin this wonderful opportunity that I had in front of me.

The problem was I still didn't understand how this worked, and I was frustrated that I didn't know what my purpose was. I thought it was just something that everyone automatically knew, and I was frustrated that I didn't know mine and it hadn't just popped into my head. I figured it was just BS and that it wasn't for me. Then my boss came back to me again and asked if I would head up another added mobile business division that the company had in his four states. I was barely holding myself together and there was more responsibility and stress coming at me. I knew I needed to get this figured out and I knew I needed help.

Looking for help

Luckily, I knew exactly who I needed to reach out to. I had an opportunity a few months before to spend time with the person who had led the intensive meeting that my supervisor had been In. She had been in town for meetings and wasn't able to fly out till the day after and I was offered the chance to spend a few hours with her. The short time I was able to spend with her in a group setting with others didn't disappoint and I became more curious about purpose and how it could help me be a better leader and person. That time only made me thirst more to find my purpose to grow as a better leader. So, without further hesitation I called her and asked her for help.

Finding my purpose

Thankfully she immediately was there for me and graciously agreed to help me. I'm sure she heard the desperation and seriousness in my voice and my excitement to find something that would help me. She took the time to lead me through finding my purpose and I am eternally grateful to her for helping me. Just like everything else in my life, it wasn't a eureka moment where suddenly I figured everything out and instantly my life changed. As a matter of fact, when it didn't instantly come to me, I was frustrated. However, she took the time as was patient and led me through the journey to help me discover it. Her help was a key to showing me the road to discovery. But the most important part was my own self-reflection and quiet time in my own head that I finally figured out.

Reflecting on my life and my career, I am truly happiest when I am helping others and helping to make people and things better. No matter if it's a business, a car, or the kitchen pantry at home, I like improving things for people. Realizing that and reflecting on the fact that I am at my happiest when I am helping people, it gave me a new perspective. So, when things are getting me frustrated at work, I need to take a moment to reflect on the bigger picture. I'm not just someone who is taking tasks and completing them, which is how I felt before. No, I am living out my purpose by helping people and improving situations. When I take the time to realize that the anger and frustration goes away.

The reason that I felt so lost when I had been fired is because I had lost my identity. Without my job or title, I didn't have an identity and didn't know who I was. That's because I didn't have a purpose. I was just a guy who handled tasks and did a job. So, when I lost my job, I had no identity because I had no purpose. Had I realized my purpose then, I would not have been as devastated by losing my job. The reason being that no one can take my purpose away. Maybe the venue would have changed but not who I was. This was a defining moment for me because when I finally realized this, it changed my way of thinking. No longer would I feel that my worth was tied to my job as my job wasn't totally within my control. This is how finding my purpose helped me strategically if you will.

Finding purpose also helped me tactically on the day to day as well. In the past when I was pressured, I would automatically react and get angry when I was stressed. Reacting that way would only make matters worse because people don't know why you are angry, they just know you are acting like a jerk. The key is taking what I call is a "leadership pause." All that means is that you need to take a short pause between whatever is stressing you and your reaction to it. Too often in the past my reaction was immediate and regrettable. Now if I receive information that stresses me, I take no immediate action. Instead, I take a walk, grab a coffee, or anything to build some time in so that I have an opportunity to address it in a calm manner. By no means am I perfect but by changing how I handle things I have improved drastically by getting my emotions in check.

Reliving

As I wrote this chapter, I could feel that some of the emotions of these past experiences of mine still run deep. However, my object by reliving them is that hearing them may help you in your own life and career situations. That falls in line with my purpose, as thinking about this time in my life Is still painful. However, by sharing them with you, my hope is that these lessons will help others without the pain that I paid for them. Looking back, I am thankful for everything that happened as it led me to a better place. Today I have the honor of leading approximately forty shops and still the mobile business in four states. Had it not have gone this way, I wouldn't be where I am today or be able to share how God led my through.

MY PERFECT SHOP

I have certainly had a long and interesting career. If you count the time when I first stepped into my dad's shop, it was the late 1970's. When I was in grade school and high school, I spent every summer and any Saturday or day off that I could in the shop. I have gone from seeing heavy gas guzzling behemoths to today's light and technology packed vehicles. I have seen a relatively small family run business to a vast network of corporate owned body shops. Thanks to being in the field for an insurance company for three years, I have seen fast shops and slow shops and everything in between. I'd like to take this chapter to reflect on what I have seen and learned in these many years in the business from both an industry and a shop level. It seems crazy for me to say it, but I have seen this business evolve from the 1970's, 1980's, 1990's, 2000's, 2010's into the 2020's.

Culture

Before we talk about the physical layout, let's talk about the intangibles and the culture I want the business to have. The first example of culture that I saw as an example was my father's business. Times may be different, but the same core group of people worked in that shop for my entire childhood. It was a close group of people that not only worked together but also chose to socialize together as well. My fondest memories are around the holidays at my dad's shop. Around Thanksgiving my dad would make sure that everyone had a turkey for their table. That act of kindness for his employees has stuck with me all these years later. It wasn't something he had to do but year in and year out his employees had turkey for their families because it was important to him.

My absolute favorite time growing up though was Christmas. First at some point, usually in December, there would be a shop Christmas party. It was always held at a catering venue and all employees and friends and vendors were invited and their spouses. I have fond memories of these parties and seeing everyone there. My favorite day though was Christmas Eve. I would be off from school that day and would always come to work with my dad. Usually, the shop would close around twelve and all the employees would sit down and have lunch together in the office. This was also a different time, and the liquor bottles would come out as well in case someone wanted to toast to the holidays, which they did. This would go on for a few hours and we would usually be home in time to get set up for Christmas Eve dinner. The office stayed set up that way for New Year's Eve as well where usually the same format would follow of everyone spending time together as a work family.

These are some of the happiest memories of my life. As I think back, I have nothing but fond thoughts of those times and all the people. It just seemed like a smaller world back then and the people in the shop knew and cared for each other in a way that is hard to replicate today. There were also company football and softball games where everyone came to enjoy themselves with their families. We didn't have phones to stare at all the time and I'm thankful that we were able to enjoy time with each other. Finally, my dad always enjoyed fishing, and he was his happiest when he was out on the water. I cannot count how many times there were fishing trips with people from the shop. If I could pick what culture I would want for my perfect shop this would be it. Where everyone is like family and chooses to spend time together because they want to.

The Team

What it comes down to is being focused on people. I just wrote several paragraphs on how important the people who work for the business are. Today it seems that modern businesses are focused more on slogans and posters on the wall than caring. It's not a slogan or a poster that means anything. It's how people feel that matters, and you won't have to put it on a wall. The poster may say we care for our people but when you don't listen to your people or give them what they need then you're lying to yourself and to them. Unfortunately, I've seen this a lot in my career, and when it's pointed out that the culture isn't what the owner or corporate office thinks it is, it is met with anger or ignorance. It seems simple but if you listen to your people and give them what they need and expect, most times that's more than enough. Sometimes just listening and hearing someone out, even if you cannot help them, is enough.

Another sad fact of business today that has been lost is love and appreciation for the customer. In today's direct repair world, customers just show up magically and didn't truly have to be "earned." I don't think anyone means anything by it, they just don't understand and appreciate how much that customer means and sometimes they are viewed as a burden. This isn't just in the collision business. I'm sure each of us has bad examples of customer service. I know I'm so appreciative when someone just shows me a little bit of customer service. How does Chick Fil-a do it anyway, where everything is their pleasure. Just having someone smile and look happy to see you makes a world of difference in your day.

The Customer

So, in my perfect shop, not only the teammates but also the customers will know and feel appreciated from the moment they walk in. Whether it's on the phone or in person, the customer will know how much they are valued and appreciated and will feel like they are the only customer we are focused on. Our availability to the customer will always be right now. Without the customer we are nothing, so we will treat them as the valued individual they are. We will also remember that in addition to repairing the vehicle, we need to repair the customer too. An accident is a confusing and intimidating situation, and we will work to help our customers through that time as well as fixing their vehicle.

Just like many other businesses, the collision business needs to evolve and make things as easy as possible for the customer. That should include pickup and delivery of their vehicle and easy access to filling out paperwork online or on their phone. Appointments should be set for drop off not only with customer convenience in mind but also the ability of the shop to be solely focused on the customer. We shouldn't be surprised or annoyed when the customer walks in, we should be overjoyed.

Would it kill us to have a smile on our face as we are greeting the customer and hand them our card and a bottle of water? Of course not. Would it be too difficult to be the customer's trusted advisor as we explain how the whole process works and what they can expect, since we do this every day. This first moment of truth is invaluable to helping to fix the customer in addition to the vehicle. Most times the shop focuses on the insurance company and the car, while the actual vehicle owner isn't focused on as much as they deserve to be.

The customer and their safety should be the PRIMARY concern. All decisions that are made throughout the repair process should be balanced against what is right for the customer and the customer's safety. Don't be confused about who the customer is. It is the vehicle owner; the insurance company is an involved third party, but they are not the customer. A business will not fail if they focus on their customers and their satisfaction.

Facility

I have worked in many different kinds and styles of shop, and many different areas too. The most difficult ones tended to be in the city and had little or no parking. However, if you were able to master running a shop without a parking lot, it helped to make you a better operator. So that if you did have the luxury of a parking lot you would be appreciative of it. Here is the reason: when you don't have a parking lot there is nowhere to "hide" cars. You had to be better, faster, and more aggressive because you can't just park cars everywhere and not expect the neighbors and the local police to be upset. You had to keep things moving and deliver vehicles, not park them and wait for something. That said the building design can make your life harder if it doesn't have a natural flow.

An example of this would be a shop with a door or doors only on one side where everything gets packed in one end, and everything needs to get moved to get vehicles out. You can still be successful but it's going to take someone jockeying and moving cars in an out to be effective. You certainly don't want your technicians to waste their time and putting their tools down to move cars around. Remember this, if your technicians aren't working on vehicles, they aren't making money, and neither are you. This chapter is titled "My Perfect Shop," and in my perfect shop the facility is designed to have a natural flow.

The two best designed shops that I ever had the opportunity to operate were both rectangles and were designed to have vehicles move in a circle through the shop. There is no point to packing vehicles in a shop because most times not all of them are being worked on, plus you must move a bunch of vehicles to get things moving. Remember this, if it's not being worked on, it shouldn't be inside the shop. The shop is reserved for vehicles actively being worked on not sitting there. The design of what to put in that circle is unique to whatever building you are dealing with, but the key is to have a balanced operation.

The main shop area will flow in a circular fashion. Vehicles will come in one area and flow from being disassembled into the body area. They will then flow into paint and paint correction. Finally, to reassembly and out to detail. There will be sub areas outside of the main circle for planning, Pre pulling, and final QC. Lean practices will be kept in mind when the shop is setup. Everything will have a defined space, and everyone will clearly know where that equipment or supply belongs.

Balance

The key to running a successful body shop and most likely most businesses is balance. The key to running a successful operation is ensuring that each facet of your business is balanced and not lacking or overworking in any area. Imagine your shop as a factory with different departments. There are raw materials coming in the front door, and finished products being delivered out of the back door. You need to have enough raw materials in the front to equal the amount of completed product in the back. Too much coming in the front which cannot be processed will only back up and create unneeded inventory. Too little raw material coming in the front won't allow you to produce enough completed product. Both what is coming in and what is going out must be balanced.

One of the key factors in figuring out how much raw material the operation requires is knowing how much material each department can handle. In the example of a body shop you have several operations within the main operation that you need to consider. In a well-organized shop, you have the following departments: Disassembly, Estimating, and parts procurement, structural and body repair, refinishing, reassembly, and cleanup. You need to know how many vehicles each of these departments can produce. What good is bringing in ten vehicles per day, if you can only disassemble and estimate five per day? What happens if every day four vehicles cannot be processed in any of the departments, but you have another ten coming in tomorrow. What happens is the line backs up, and your system is out of balance. What you should be bringing in cannot exceed the lowest department number that you can produce. Again, if I can only paint four vehicles per day, I shouldn't be bringing in ten vehicles per day as there will be a bottleneck in paint.

Dropoff

As I mentioned, paperwork should be filled out electronically beforehand. However, with the customer at your facility not only is it time to win them over as a promoter. It is also the time to go over their vehicle with them. As silly as this sounds it doesn't always happen. Who is better than the customer to tell you and show you live, their concerns. What better time would there be to show the customer any concerns that you have about their vehicle.

Now is the time to dial in and get all the information you need to about the vehicle, what happened, and any potential issues you see. If there is a problem or an issue, it needs to be identified now and not when the vehicle has been repaired and is ready to be delivered. After going over everything, including what happened and what the customer has noticed as being damaged, you can also note damage that is not included in this loss and that we can offer to provide additional pricing for those items.

The last thing you need to do before the customer leaves is set the expectation for what comes next. This is your opportunity to build trust with the customer by showing them they can depend on you to be truthful with them. An example might be telling the customer you will call them at 10am tomorrow to follow up with them. That's an easy enough promise, but now you need to come through and do it. So, by calling the customer when you told them you would, you build trust and show the customer you will come through with what you say. The customer is now free to go on their way.

Planning

Once the customer is gone, we need to start planning out how we are going to repair their vehicle. Repair decisions and methodology need to be made by the repair experts and that is the shop. The vehicle should be thoroughly photo'd in its current virgin state as we have received it. Secondly, the vehicle should be washed. There are many reasons for this, including the ability to clearly see all the damage. This is especially true in the winter months when salt and dirt cover the car. While the vehicle is in prewash, the estimator should start building their initial estimate and pulling repair procedures for the vehicle. This planning stage is critical, and all repair or replacement decisions should be made with factory procedures in hand. This is also the time where the pre-scanning should be done so that the estimator can review and plan the repair with the vehicle's pre scan already completed.

With that in mind, and a now clean vehicle, we can continue the planning process. In the shop there will be a well-lit and dedicated place for us to continue our check-in. In this bay, which should not be in the main shop production area, we will take more photos and begin our mapping process. We will use various markers to write on the vehicle and identify all damage. This mapping will be so detailed that no technician will need to ask any questions as all the details will be there and explain everything. If someone needs to ask a question, we fail in our mission. There should never be a time when a technician needs to put their tools down and come looking for someone to get a question answered. We will also place the printed-out procedures that we think we will need as well as a copy of the preliminary estimate, and the insurance assignment.

As I mentioned, this area will be well lit, should have access to a scissor lift, as well as portable lights to focus on damage and mirrors and line boards, and other tools to be able to properly document damage. It would also be a good idea to have a recorded video system in this area. The reason for this would be to be able to go back to the video if there is a question or damage that needs to proven further. As part of the planning process each vehicle will have an intake video taken by the estimator and narrated of what they see, both inside and outside of the vehicle. This area is a separate and dedicated area and is used only for this purpose. It especially needs to be available in times of darkness or inclement weather.

Pre repair

The next area of our shop that the vehicle will go to is the pre repair area. Here we will have a frame machine available for pre-pulling damage and measuring vehicles. Short of a scratch or ding, every vehicle that has sustained accidental damage should be measured to identify structural damage. Having the ability to pull here will also enable us to properly identify all the damage that may have otherwise be missed. This will also enable us to judge the repairability of panels by enabling us to see how panels look after they are rough pulled. If a vehicle is drivable and there is the possibility of suspension damage, a pre alignment will be performed in house if equipped or at a sublet vendor.

Surgical Disassembly

Our goal here is to find, document, and write for all the damage that occurred in the loss and to ascertain everything needed to properly repair this vehicle. This area will be a dedicated area specifically set aside for this purpose. The technicians in this area will only be responsible for the disassembly of the vehicles. This area will also be well lit and will have scissor lifts for the vehicles. Each disassembler will be matched with an estimator. The estimators will have their desks in the shop right at these disassembly bays.

For the production shop that I am thinking of, there will be a minimum of three disassemblers and three estimators in three bays with 3 scissor lifts. The bays will be equipped with tool carts and toolboxes for these technicians, so they don't need to go anywhere to get anything. There will so be supplies of gallon, and sandwich sized bags. There will also be supplies to cover and protect interiors and vehicles with no glass or doors. The shop will also need an ample supply of part carts as the cart or carts will be slaved to that vehicle as long as it is in the shop.

When the vehicle comes into this area, the first thing that happens is the estimator and the tech go over the paperwork in the vehicle and the vehicle mapping. Next the technician carefully and methodically takes the vehicle apart. A technique called micro bagging is applied. For instance, a large bag is used for the left front door. Within that bag are smaller bags for all the components that attach to that door. Large components such as interior trim panels are put inside of large trash bags for protection and are put in a secure area or attached to the part cart. Each bag is clearly marked with a sharpie on what it contains, and photos are taken by the estimator as the vehicle is taken apart. The purpose for that is both to identify damage and aid in the reassembly of the vehicle. There will be a procedure for how to place parts on the parts cart. Broken parts that need to be replaced will be on the bottom of the cart. Parts that will be re-installed after they are checked for damage will be on the upper shelves of the cart.

As the vehicle is taken apart, any questions that arise are addressed by the senior technician and senior painter.

The estimator can also continue to write a proper estimate and download any additional procedures necessary with the disassembly tech. Vehicles are fully disassembled as needed as are the components. If a bumper is destroyed, not only is the bumper taken off the vehicle. All components that attach to that bumper are also taken off and bagged and tagged. All parts are removed from the vehicle until all, and I mean all the damage is uncovered. The head painter is consulted on the color and decisions on what blending of panels is needed is decided now. Blend panels are also fully disassembled including all trim items that need to be removed.

Any moldings that will be re-used will also be cleaned and retaped now to make sure that they can be. There will be a supply of clips and fasteners in this area as well. That way, any needed clips are documented and sourced and charged for now. Just like we already cleaned and retaped other moldings, these moldings will have the clips attached and ready to go. This system will also have the capabilities to invoice for the clips and items needed. Any consumables needed and in what quantity will also be decided here. Since we have the procedures and we know what panels need to be replaced, we can accurately measure what quantities of consumables are needed and charge accordingly for them. The 3M online system along with the proper ability to measure the quantities needed will be utilized. If a stripe tape is called for, the stripe tape will be sourced and measured now, and the appropriate amount will be put inside of the vehicle or attached to the part cart.

At this point we should have a fully disassembled vehicle. As I mentioned all damage needs to be uncovered and the vehicle needs to be taken apart so that no additional damage is possible. This includes removing condensers, radiators, fans, and anything else that may be damaged. The disassembler will be equipped with needed tools to close off coolant and transmission lines so that vehicles can be moved around without dripping all over the floor. If panels need to be cut off to inspect for further damage, we can also do that now as well. This is also the time to order, source and charge for any needed fluids such as transmission fluid or the proper antifreeze. These items need to go on the parts cart as well. If glass needs to be removed, it is removed now and the proper consumables are ordered, sourced, and charged for. Glasses and mating surfaces are cleaned and prepped now to prevent future damage or a problem when it comes to re-assembling the vehicle.

Gatekeeping

The estimate is reviewed with the estimator, disassemblers, senior tech, and painter. There will be a collaborative approach, and the team needs to all agree and sign off on repairs. The vehicle mapping needs to be checked and updated if needed. The estimate and procedures are checked again and signed off on, this includes information and procedure on calibrations. The vehicle is protected from the elements and any openings and wiring is protected and documented. The part cart is then checked to ensure everything is up to standards as well. The parts are sourced from the proper vendors and are followed up on to ensure they are available. Only after the vehicle, the part cart, and the paperwork are all signed off on, is the vehicle ready to move out of this area.

At this point we should be able to report back to our customer how long the vehicle repairs will generally take. While we are waiting for parts, we will seek out what other things we can do to move repairs along while we wait. If there is wheel repair or other sublet items that can be done, will we do them now. If there is suspension or mechanical work that needs to be done, we will prioritize that work and do it now if we can. Another consideration if the vehicle is structurally damaged is to have something that Sterling Autobody used to call "Random Reduction." Any vehicle that has sustained structural damage goes to our senior technician. That technician is responsible for measuring and pulling all vehicles with structural damage. That technician can also cut out the damaged structure, and setup the new part in place. So that when he or she is finished with it, the part installation can be finished by a lessor experienced tech.

The whole idea here is speed and accuracy. Most vehicles in a conventional shop sit idle most of the time with no one working on them. Also because of inefficiency and inaccuracy, the vehicle is often stopped for missing parts and missing damage. In my perfect shop we will spend more time in the beginning of the process than a conventional shop does. However, this will pay dividends later in the processes as vehicles will move unhindered through the process in a predictable and defined manner. Speeding though these critical steps is a recipe for disaster and causes frustration, poor quality, and inefficiency. For some reason for conventional shops this is an extreme difference in thinking. However, once a shop commits to the discipline of doing things this way, they will never want to go back to the old way of doing things. Also, we will not be wasting our experienced technicians time and knowledge by having them complete tasks that a less seasoned tech can be completing.

Keep in mind that the vehicle just dropped off today or yesterday and we are this far in the process. For a small job of a bumper and fender replacement, the vehicle is ready for painting as soon as those parts arrive. If there are panels that need to be repaired, and if we can repair them without the aid of parts that are on order, we can do that now. The goal is to "jump" the system and get the vehicle to the furthest department we can, as fast and safely as we can. So, in this way, a vehicle can go from drop off to being technically in the paint department in a manner of hours. A job like this can be cycled in the shop in two or three days as opposed to much longer, which is the norm for many conventional shops today.

Parts

Another key to being able to run an efficient shop like this is a strong and process driven parts department. Much of the downtime in today's conventional shops comes from a poor process and waiting for or never having ordered the proper parts.

The people responsible for parts are incredibly important to the success of the operations. The first key in this department is ensuring that all needed parts have been ordered and that they follow up consistently with any parts that we are waiting for. If a vehicle is just sitting and waiting and not being worked on, this is dead time that is not doing the business or the customer any good. So, this department's first mission is to ensure accuracy and timeliness.

Secondly the receipt of the correct parts is of paramount importance. All boxes and packages must be opened and carefully checked against the original parts aka "mirror matching." This sounds simple and it is, but I have seen too many unopened boxes and packages than I care to mention. Today's vehicles come in many different styles and variations. There may be six different styles of bumper and different moldings and lamps as well. A detailed and careful inspection is necessary to ensure we have the correct and undamaged parts. Until this has been done if you are going to assume anything you need to assume you have the wrong parts. Once the correct parts have arrived, they need to be carefully staged on the part cart or carts. The same is true for large parts and sheet metal. If needed, the parts department will collaborate with the body tech to ensure the correct parts have arrived. Only after this process is completed and checked will the vehicle be flagged as ready for production. Parts cannot be stacked up and scattered all over the place. They all need to be on carefully checked and marked parts carts. Too much time gets wasted in conventional shops walking around and looking for things. A neat and organized parts department, and carts organized to match the vehicle cannot be beaten.

Ready for Production

Now the vehicle is ready to continue its journey through the shop. By following this process, you will clearly see these vehicles will move more quickly and in a more predicable manner than a conventional shop. We will not have the frustrations and the back and forth and missed promises that a conventional shop will have. The body technician should have all the parts they require. They should have a clean and clearly marked vehicle telling them what to do. They should have a vehicle that is measured and pulled as needed as well. Anything that may cause them problems should have already been eliminated. The actual time taken in the body shop should be for actual work and not for mistakes, problems or waiting for things.

When the body tech is finished the repairs, they should sign off on their work and double check that all their work is up to the proper standards as well as procedures being followed along with the manager. The tech should also ensure that all necessary parts are in hand for the vehicle to be disassembled. Before the vehicle is sent to paint, the mechanical components such as cooling, air conditioning etc should be installed and the vehicle should be in fully running and checked condition before moving into the paint department. Also, if any other components can be built now and be made ready for installation that should also be done now. An example of this would be a chrome truck bumper that needed to be replaced. We should take the time now to install the components that we took off the original bumper and install them on the replacement bumper. There also could be things like lamps that we may need to put together and install bulbs etc, we should do that now. Another example is doors and tailgates. They will be built with everything we can, except for anything that needs to be left off for the painting process. Don't wait until the vehicle is painted to find any problems.

Paint Department

The paint department is commonly recognized as a bottleneck as there are only so many booth cycles you can run in a day. However, there are things you can do to maximize your efficiency. Examples of this can be batching part booth runs where you put the parts for several jobs at once in the booth and effectively paint several cars in one booth cycle. A key to this is thinking through the vehicles you must paint or even the different colors that can be batched together. It makes sense to take blend panels off vehicles if they can be batched and painted together now instead of stacking up in front of the booth. The paint booth is a precious commodity and should never be sitting idle and should never be used for anything other than painting. Sanding and masking should always be done outside of the booth and the booth should be used and reserved for painting only. Not only that but it should always be kept in clean and pristine condition. The booth is the most expensive piece of equipment in the shop and should be respected and treated as such. The same holds true for the paint mixing room and it should be always kept clean and bright.

All vehicles that arrive in the paint shop today should be primed today so that they can cure overnight. In those cases where that isn't possible infrared technology, or other technology should be used to cure the primer. But before that the painter needs to check the body work and parts that came over with the vehicle and sign off on them for quality. Care should always be taken to properly sand and block bodywork. The goal is speed if it is coupled with quality. The painter needs to take the proper amount of time to mix colors and tint where applicable. Once the vehicles and parts are painted and cured the paint staff will be responsible for finish corrections. There is no reason to move the vehicle forward in the process if there are paint defects. These should be handled as soon as possible in the paint shop and by the paint staff. Only after these corrections have been made can the vehicle be signed off on by the paint staff and the vehicle move ahead in the process.

Just like the shop has disassemblers who are responsible for the taking apart of vehicles, we will also have dedicated reassembly technicians who only reassemble. Remember at this point everything is painted and prebuilt so the reassembly technicians' task should not be difficult. The work that we did in the beginning of the process should continue to show dividends now. Remember that we micro bagged, tagged, and took photos of everything. We even had cleaned and retaped and pre clipped everything we needed too. Once a vehicle is painted it should be easy for us to predict when the vehicle is going to be ready for delivery as we took away many if not all the "mulligans" that could have come up to bite us. Instead of stop and start, our vehicles should race to the finish. Doing things this way should also ease tensions and frustrations and vehicles should move without everyone being frustrated. Once the vehicle is fully assembled and the final check in this department is done, we still have a few more steps to take.

Final steps

The parts carts we used need to be checked, emptied, and cleaned off and returned to be ready for another vehicle. Our fully assembled vehicle now goes to another dedicated area where we will do final quality control and ADAS calibrations. This dedicated space will be well lit and only used for these purposes. The manager or production manager will print out the final estimate and check each area of the vehicle that we worked on and ensure that the final post scan of the vehicle is also completed. Any ADAS calibrations will be taken care of in this area. Once the manager has checked off that everything has been completed to our quality standards, all vehicles will be taken on a test drive. Once the test drive is completed and passed the vehicle will go to our cleanup department. The vehicle will be fully cleaned inside and out and will be dressed and ready for the customer.

Final Thoughts

From a customer's perspective this has been an easy, painless, and predictable process. We asked in the beginning how the customer wanted to be kept informed, and we delivered on their ask. Since we took the proper amount of time in the beginning of the process, we eliminated problems that pop up during the process so that the vehicle continued to move to completion without slowing down or interruptions. We are ready to deliver them a quality product on time and as promised. Once you operate a shop this way and see for yourself how much faster and less stressful it flows, you will never want to go back to a conventional shop. It makes no sense to speed through the beginning of the process only to hit multiple roadblocks later that force you to stop and wait and miss your promises to your customer. I saw for myself how much better things flow this way, and now much less stress the employees and customers feel.

The Extra Mile

Culture is Key

Employees who choose to socialize together probably work in a good culture

The customer is the focus

Set your shop up for success with lean and a circular flow

Balance is paramount

Spend more time planning and it will save you time in the end

Surgical disassembly identifies everything up front

Mirror match parts

Gatekeep before you start working on the repair

Quality throughout

Batch jobs to beat the bottleneck in paint

EPILOGUE

One thing that I have learned on my journey from single unit management to multi-unit management is that growth and change are important. What made you successful as a single unit manager is not what is going to help you to be successful in multi-unit management.

Without the challenges, failures, and growth opportunities mentioned within this book I would not have been able to suceed in going from one, to eight, to forty units. In addition to that, I also learned to be flexible so that when new challenged arose, I didn't self destruct. Finding and remembering my purpose was a ket factor to making this jump.

I won't lie to you, multi unit management is not easy, especially for a former control freak and doer like me. This journey has taught me patience, and the leadership skills that I needed to grow into. Leadership is the most important skill that you can work on in yourself. Our world today is sadly lacking leaders. Especially other focused leaders. Our world, our work, and our comunities desperately need leaders.

What's stopping you?

www.ingramcontent.com/pod-product-compliance
Lightning Source LLC
Chambersburg PA
CBHW050304230526
45471CB00005B/2008